Indie Socks

Knitting Patterns and Dyer Profiles
Featuring Hand-Dyed Yarns

by
Chrissy Gardiner

with dyer profiles by
Donna Arney

SYDWILLOW PRESS

PORTLAND, OR

D1373688

354774G

Indie Socks
Knitting Patterns and Dyer Profiles Featuring Hand-Dyed Yarns

First Edition

Sydwillow Press
P.O. Box 13607
Portland, OR 97213

www.sydwillowpress.com

Dyer profiles by Donna Arney
Photographs by Gail Marracci
Book design by Janel Laidman and Chrissy Gardiner
Cover design by David Sparks
Author photo by Rosemary Ragusa

Printed in China by Asia Pacific Offset Ltd.

ISBN: 978-0-9819668-1-6

10 9 8 7 6 5 4 3 2 1

For Sydney and Owen.
Thanks for the never-ending inspiration
and constant distraction.

Acknowledgements

There were many people involved in the production of this book.

I'd like to thank my family, for putting up with the yarn, the late nights and the frequent complaining.

I'd like to thank my business partner and dyer profile author, Donna, who, in addition to writing, organized many, many things behind the scenes and certainly made my job much easier.

I'd like to thank all the awesome indie dyers who filled out questionnaires, sent yarn, and supported this project from the beginning.

I'd like to thank my amazing photographer, Gail, who spent several Saturdays crawling around on the ground to get the perfect shot of my feet. This was particularly fun in 35-degree weather.

Looking down over Manzanita, Oregon, where much of this book was written and formatted.

I'd like to thank my friend and fellow author, Janel Laidman, for helping to lay the groundwork for this book's interior design, as well as my friend and neighbor, David Sparks, for his amazing cover design.

I'd like to thank my mom, Janet Orjala, for her editing assistance and constant encouragement.

I'd like to thank my amazing technical editors, Amy Polcyn and Amanda Woodruff, for ferreting out as many errors as humanly possible.

I'd like to thank my test knitters, Michelle, Erynne, Deb, Alice, Carol S., Crystal, Dustina, Lain, Kirsten, Nan, Carol B., Ariel, Anastasia and Beth, for all their hard work ensuring the patterns make sense to actual knitters.

I'd like to thank Cat Bordhi and all the Visionaries for their continual encouragement and support.

And finally, I'd like to thank you, the knitters, for using this book. After all, that's what it's for!

Table of Contents

Introduction

Hello. My name is Chrissy Gardiner, and I am addicted to socks. If you're reading this, there's a good chance you are, too. You may have already met me somewhere along the path to sock addiction, perhaps via one of my sock patterns in Interweave Knits, Twist Collective or Knitty. You may have learned to share my obsession with toe-up socks when you picked up a copy of my first book, *Toe-Up! Patterns and Worksheets to Whip Your Sock Knitting Into Shape*.

If you are an old friend, it's good to see you again. If this is the first time our paths have crossed, it's great to meet you! I am sure that we will be great compatriots in sock knitting and have had lots of fun together by the time we reach the end of this book. Tally ho!

I was inspired to write this book after visiting the marketplace of the great sock knitters' gathering, Sock Summit, in 2009. At the time, I was designing mainly for my pattern line, which was then exclusively sold in local yarn shops. I needed to use widely-available commercial yarns that were stocked at those shops or they'd have little interest in carrying my patterns.

As much as I loved the yarns I was able to work with, I felt a little like I was missing out on a big chunk of the fun stuff that was going on with the explosion of tiny indie dyers, and I thought that writing a book to highlight a few of those dyers would give me a chance to explore these yarns and the culture behind them in a way I don't often get to in my regular design career.

My business partner, Donna (she's the one who conducted the interviews and wrote up the profiles of our featured dyers), and I started kicking around dyer names and quickly ended up with a huge list of people we wanted to feature in the book.

Obviously we couldn't include everyone, so we whittled the list down to 24 dyers whom we felt represented a broad cross-section of the industry, from one-woman operations, to larger companies who have been hand-dyeing yarn for years and are well-known to many knitters. I'll talk a little bit more about our selection process in the section on indie dyers.

The CSK

As the nugget of an idea for this book was knocking around in my head, I decided I needed a new way to keep myself on track, as well as a fun way to involve knitters in its creation. My fellow author and designer, Miriam Felton, used the metaphor of "like a

CSA, but for books" when describing her idea for releasing patterns ahead of an actual printed book. Donna and I had already kicked around the idea of finding investors who wanted to help fund production of the book, but the thought of selling 'shares' to individual knitters was a definite light-bulb moment. When I mentioned the CSA analogy to my husband, he exclaimed "it's not a CSA, it's a CSK! As in, 'Community Supported Knitting'." Thus, the idea for the Indie Socks CSK was formed.

I started taking subscriptions for the CSK in early June of 2010, right before leaving for vacation (one of my more brilliant ideas, as I left Donna to field the flood of sign-ups while I was sequestered without internet access in the wilds of the Adirondacks), and the first pattern was released in August.

Every month thereafter, through July 2011, a new design was released to the 250+ members of the CSK (you'll see these designs indicated throughout the book). The CSK was a blast, with an active Ravelry group, fun raffle prize drawings and a get-together at Sock Summit 2011. Thank you so much to all of my investors – this book may not have happened without you!

How to use this book…

Unlike *Toe-Up!*, this book is not focused on instruction. I've tried to include most of the basic information you'll need in the glossary of techniques at the back, but I'm assuming that you have a basic foundation of sock knitting techniques.

Look for the *Tips & Tricks* sections sprinkled throughout the book for a few of my favorite sock knitting techniques and further discussion of working with color.

If you run into something that's unfamiliar to you, I'd suggest conducting a quick internet search or checking out www.knittinghelp.com for answers. You can also contact me via e-mail at info@sydwillowpress.com with questions, or join our group on Ravelry by going to www.ravelry.com/groups/indie-socks-csk. You'll need a free Ravelry account to join, but if you don't already have one, you really should get one! Ravelry is an amazing resource for any knitter.

As you flip through the patterns, you'll see they're divided into three sections. The first, "Mild Yarns", utilizes semi-solid yarns in gentle colors that are very easy to work with. These patterns may be slightly more complex, because the nature of the colorways allows a bit more leeway in the stitch patterns.

The middle section, "Flavorful Yarns", focuses on mild to moderately variegated yarns in light to medium shades, allowing some play with stitch patterns. These yarns are slightly more of a challenge to work with, but they are still moderately forgiving.

The final pattern section, "Spicy Yarns", includes patterns for the most challenging yarns I was sent to work with. These are high-contrast and/or dark yarns that tend to obscure stitch patterns and can really drive you crazy if you don't know a few tricks for pounding them into submission. I cover some of these tricks on p. 109, and you'll see them out in full force in these patterns.

I hope this book provides you with inspiration and loads of knitting fun while taking some of the guesswork out of buying and using hand-dyed yarn.

Working with Hand-Dyed Yarn

Choosing Yarn

What's the best way to go about buying yarn from an indie dyer? Many of us have giant stashes of lovely variegated yarn that we just couldn't resist because of the alluring colors, but now that we've got it home, we have no idea what to do with it.

Variegated yarn is the signature of many indie dyers because it is so eye-catching. However, it's also very challenging to work with (and the wilder the colors, the more difficult it is to find a project that will highlight both yarn and pattern).

Any knitter who has spent some time working with variegated yarn will have his or her share of horror stories about yarn-and-pattern combinations gone wrong.

There are a few questions to ask yourself when determining what kind of hand-dyed yarn will best suit your personal knitting style.

Do you prefer complex patterns, or are you just as content knitting something simple and letting the yarn do all the work?

Do you get frustrated when a yarn obscures a pattern, or are you happy to enjoy the process of knitting a particular pattern even if it's over-shadowed by the yarn in the end?

Do you gravitate toward deep, saturated colors or are you delighted by subtler, lighter hues?

Do you delight in extreme variegation or are semi-solids more your style?

The answers to these questions can lead you toward a more practical method of choosing yarns to purchase. Let's tackle them one at a time.

1) Complex vs. Simple

If you are a simple pattern knitter, you've got an easier road ahead of you. Variegated yarns generally work very well with simple patterns because there isn't a complex web of cables, lace or texture to fight with the coloration of the yarn.

If you're happy knitting stockinette or basic ribbed socks, you can choose any yarn you'd like to work with and not have to worry too much about the results. Your main concern will be limiting pooling or flashing, if it bothers you. Again, this is a personal style decision and there is no reason to avoid pooling or flashing unless it really doesn't appeal to you.

On the other hand, if you're bored silly

by stockinette or ribbed socks, you'll need to select your yarn and pattern combination more carefully.

As a general rule, lighter colors will show off stitch patterns better than darker colors. Semi-solids will handle complex designs better than intensely variegated yarns, but if you must have some variegation, yarns with similar color values (relative lightness or darkness) will highlight a pattern better than yarns with very different color values (for example, a black-and-white striped yarn).

One easy way to determine if a yarn's colors are similar in value is to take a black-and-white photo of it. If the yarn looks solid (or nearly so) in the photo, the colors are similar in value. If it looks striped in the photo, the colors have different values and will be more of a challenge to work with.

The more complex the pattern, the lower the tolerance for large color variations or dark colors.

2) To Obscure or Not To Obscure
Here is an area where personal style preference very much comes into play. Your answer will be different depending on whether you are a process knitter (one who knits for the pure joy of knitting, with the end product a nice side benefit) or a product knitter (one who knits mainly to produce an awe-inspiring end product).

Some knitters (usually product knitters) are endlessly annoyed by yarns that don't highlight complex stitch patterns, wondering why anyone would do all that work only to end up with a sock that barely shows the design unless examined very closely.

Other knitters (you process folks) want socks made from a certain yarn, aspire to knit a certain pattern for the fun of it, and don't really care what the end result looks like.

If you don't mind your pattern potentially being obscured by your yarn, the world is your oyster – feel free to combine yarn and pattern with abandon. If you're a bit less free-wheeling and really prefer that your stitch pattern be shown to its best advantage, you'll want to review the color rules laid out in #1 above.

3) Dark vs Light
Are you someone who can't stand pastels? Are blood red, pumpkin orange, and royal blue, shades you wouldn't be caught dead in? Chances are, you have a preference for lighter or darker hues, and the yarns you gravitate toward will reflect this. If, like me, you really don't have a preference, consider yourself lucky – the wider your range of preferences, the more options you have available. On the flip side, you can end up with so many choices that it's nearly impossible to make a decision. As you'll see in #1 above, lighter shades will better show off patterns, with black (the ultimate dark color) essentially obscuring any pattern unless viewed up close.

4) Strong Variegation vs Semi-Solid
Can you guess which of these options is a better choice for showing off a complex design? You can find the answer in #1 above.

At this point, those of you who fancy your dark, saturated, crazily variegated yarns are probably feeling a little depressed, wondering if you'll ever be able to knit anything out of your favorite yarns.

Don't despair! Several of the patterns in this book were developed for yarns just like these. It can be done with great success – you just might have to do a little more work to find a pattern that works just right for your yarn.

Indie Dyers

What is an Indie Dyer?

Dictionary.com defines "indie" as "an independently owned business." In the yarn world, that encompasses just about everyone as there are very few (if any) publicly traded yarn companies. Even the giant Lion Brand Yarn Co. is a family-owned business.

For the purposes of this book, I've gone a step further and included process as well as ownership. All of our indie dyers not only own their own yarn companies, but they are also intimately involved in the production of their yarn.

These dyers all have their hands in the process of creating these lovely yarns on a daily basis rather than programming a machine to color hundreds of skeins at once in a giant vat, in an exactly reproducible hue.

Some of our dyers have been around for decades, while some are just getting started. Some of the names are recognizable to almost every knitter, and some will be new to nearly all of you. They all have fiercely loyal followings and create what I consider to be miniature works of art.

Obviously this book includes just a tiny sampling of all the great indie work that's being done out there. New businesses pop up almost daily, and occasionally the demands of dyeing yarn day after day get to be too much and a dyer will quietly close up shop. There's no guarantee that the dyers you read about in this book will still be around when we go to press (although we sure hope they are!), but fear not. There are hundreds of options available to choose from, so finding a substitute yarn should be a fun and exciting challenge.

Why are Indie Dyers Important?

With hand-dyed skeins running $20-$50 a pop, is it really worth buying yarn from indie dyers? In my opinion, absolutely!

Indies offer colors and dye techniques to appeal to nearly everyone. Prefer bright colors? Wide stripes? Pooling? No pooling? Pastels? Brights? There's sure to be an indie dyer who has just what you're looking for. Ten years ago, that wasn't necessarily the case.

You're also supporting a small business and doing your part to help the economy. Yes, I can come up with all sorts of ways to justify spending money on yarn!

Mild Yarns

Materials:

Approximately 400 yards of fingering-weight yarn. *Sample uses Alpha B Yarn Luxe B (50% merino wool, 50% silk) in 'The World Is My Oyster'.*

US1 (2.25mm) needles or size needed to obtain gauge

Yarn needle, 2 cable needles

Gauge:

8-1/2 stitches/12 rounds per inch in stockinette stitch

Size:

Foot circumference = approximately 7-1/2"

Spyglass Lane

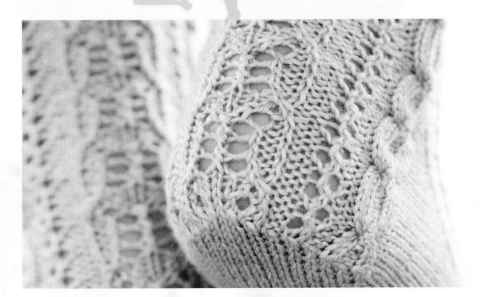

Designer's Notes:

I fell in love with this luminous semi-solid colorway on sight. Anne, the dyer behind Alpha B Yarn, is an expert at mixing incredible solid hues that provide the perfect medium for complex lace and cable work.

I decided to go nuts with this ideal background, and worked a fun cable motif down the front of the sock that reminds me of eyes (hence the name 'Spyglass Lane'), a gordian knot down the side of the leg extending along the edge of the heel flap, and one of my favorite cable-and-lace motifs, Brisket Lace, down the back of the leg. All these elements combine to make a fun-to-knit showpiece sock.

This sock would not be the best choice for a highly variegated yarn due to the complexity of the stitch patterns, but a light-to-medium solid or semi-solid should give you great results.

Special Abbreviations and Techniques for This Pattern

knot: Sl2 to cable needle and hold in back, sl2 to second cable needle and hold in front, k2, p2 from cable needle held in front, k2 from cable needle held in back

T1/1/1B: Sl2 to cable needle and hold in back, k1, [p1, k1] from cable needle

T1/1/1F: Sl1 to cable needle and hold in front, k1, p1, k1 from cable needle

Leg

Cast on 69 stitches and divide them over dpns or circular needles as follows:

- If using dpns, place 15 stitches on needle 1, 19 stitches on needle 2, 16 stitches on needle 3, and 19 stitches on needle 4.
- If using circular needle(s), place 34 stitches on needle 1 and 35 stitches on needle 2.

The first 34 stitches of the round are the instep stitches and the last 35 stitches are the heel stitches. Join stitches into round being careful not to twist. Work ribbing as follows (or from chart on p. 17):

Round 1: P2, k2, [p1, k1] 5x, p1, k4, [p1, k1] 5x, p1, k2, p2; p1, [k2, p2] 3x, [k1, p1] 4x, k1, [p2, k2] 3x, p1.

Round 2: P2, k2tog, YO, [p1, k1] 5x, p1, k4, [p1, k1] 5x, p1, YO, SSK, p2; p1, [k2, p2] 2x, k2tog, YO, p2, [k1, p1] 4x, k1, p2, YO, SSK, [p2, k2] 2x, p1.

Round 3: Repeat Round 1.

Round 4: P2, YO, SSK, [p1, k1] 5x, p1, C4B, [p1, k1] 5x, p1, k2tog, YO, p2; p1, [k2, p2] 2x, YO, SSK, p2, [k1, p1] 4x, k1, p2, k2tog, YO, [p2, k2] 2x, p1.

Round 5: Repeat Round 1.

Round 6: Repeat Round 2.

Round 7: Repeat Round 1.

Round 8: P2, YO, SSK, [p1, k1] 5x, p1, C4B, [p1, k1] 5x, p1, k2tog, YO, p2; p1, knot, p2, YO, SSK, p2, [k1, p1] 4x, k1, p2, k2tog, YO, p2, knot, p1.

Round 9: Repeat Round 1.

Round 10: Repeat Round 2.

Begin working *Instep Cable Pattern* across the 34 instep stitches, and *Back Leg Pattern* across the 35 heel stitches (charts on p. 18-19):

Instep Cable Pattern

(over 34 stitches and 32 rounds)

Round 1: P2, k2, p11, k4, p11, k2, p2.

Round 2: P2, YO, SSK, p11, C4B, p11, k2tog, YO, p2.

Round 3: Repeat Round 1.

Round 4: P2, k2tog, YO, p9, C4B, C4F, p9, YO, SSK, p2.

Round 5: P2, k2, p9, k8, p9, k2, p2.

Round 6: P2, YO, SSK, p7, T4B, C4F, T4F, p7, k2tog, YO, p2.

Round 7: P2, k2, p7, k2, p2, k4, p2, k2, p7, k2, p2.

Round 8: P2, k2tog, YO, p5, T4B, p2, k4, p2, T4F, p5, YO, SSK, p2.

Round 9: P2, k2, p5, k2, p4, k4, p4, k2, p5, k2, p2.

Round 10: P2, YO, SSK, p4, T3B, p4, C4F, p4, T3F, p4, k2tog, YO, p2.

Round 11: P2, k2, p4, k2, p5, k4, p5, k2, p4, k2, p2.

Round 12: P2, k2tog, YO, p3, T3B, p3, C4B, C4F, p3, T3F, p3, YO, SSK, p2.

Round 13: P2, k2, p3, k2, p4, k8, p4, k2, p3, k2, p2.

Round 14: P2, YO, SSK, p2, T3B, p2, T4B, k4, T4F, p2, T3F, p2, k2tog, YO, p2.

Round 15: [P2, k2] 2x, p3, k2, p2, k4, p2, k2, p3, [k2, p2] 2x.

Round 16: P2, k2tog, YO, p2, k2, p1, T4B, p2, C4B, p2, T4F, p1, k2, p2, YO, SSK, p2.

Round 17: [P2, k2] 2x, p1, k2, p4, k4, p4, k2, p1, [k2, p2] 2x.

Round 18: P2, YO, SSK, p2, k2, p1, k2, p4, k4, p4, k2, p1, k2, p2, k2tog, YO, p2.

Round 19: Repeat Round 17.

Round 20: P2, k2tog, YO, p2, k2, p1, T4F, p2, C4B, p2, T4B, p1, k2, p2, YO, SSK, p2.

Round 21: [P2, k2] 2x, p3, k2, p2, k4, p2, k2, p3, [k2, p2] 2x.

Round 22: P2, YO, SSK, p2, T3F, p2, T4F, k4, T4B, p2, T3B, p2, k2tog, YO, p2.

Round 23: P2, k2, p3, k2, p4, k8, p4, k2, p3, k2, p2.

Round 24: P2, k2tog, YO, p3, T3F, p3, T4B, p3, T3B, p3, YO, SSK, p2.
Round 25: P2, k2, p4, k2, p5, k4, p5, k2, p4, k2, p2.
Round 26: P2, YO, SSK, p4, T3F, p4, C4F, p4, T3B, p4, k2tog, YO, p2.
Round 27: P2, k2, p5, k2, p4, k4, p4, k2, p5, k2, p2.
Round 28: P2, k2tog, YO, p5, T4F, p2, k4, p2, T4B, p5, YO, SSK, p2.
Round 29: P2, k2, p7, k2, p2, k4, p2, k2, p7, k2, p2.
Round 30: P2, YO, SSK, p7, T4F, C4F, T4B, p7, k2tog, YO, p2.
Round 31: P2, k2, p9, k8, p9, k2, p2.
Round 32: P2, k2tog, YO, p9, T4F, T4B, p9, YO, SSK, p2.

Back Leg Pattern

(over 35 stitches and 20 rounds)
Round 1 (and all odd-numbered rounds): P1, [k2, p2] 3x, k1, p1, k5, p1, k1, [p2, k2] 3x, p1.
Round 2: P1, [k2, p2] 2x, YO, SSK, p2, k-tbl, p1, k-tbl, YO, SK2P, YO, k-tbl, p1, k-tbl, p2, k2tog, YO, [p2, k2] 2x, p1.
Round 4: P1, [k2, p2] 2x, k2tog, YO, p2, k-tbl, p1, k-tbl, YO, SK2P, YO, k-tbl, p1, k-tbl, p2, YO, SSK, [p2, k2] 2x, p1.
Round 6: Repeat Round 2.
Round 8: P1, knot, p2, k2tog, YO, p2, T1/1/1B, k-tbl, k1, k-tbl, T1/1/1F, p2, YO, SSK, p2, knot, p1.

Round 10: P1, [k2, p2] 2x, YO, SSK, p2, k-tbl, p1, YO, SSK, k1, k2tog, YO, p1, k-tbl, p2, k2tog, YO, [p2, k2] 2x, p1.
Round 12: P1, [k2, p2] 2x, k2tog, YO, p2, k-tbl, p1, k-tbl, YO, SK2P, YO, k-tbl, p1, k-tbl, p2, YO, SSK, [p2, k2] 2x, p1.
Round 14: P1, [k2, p2] 2x, YO, SSK, p2, k-tbl, p1, k-tbl, YO, SK2P, YO, k-tbl, p1, k-tbl, p2, k2tog, YO, [p2, k2] 2x, p1.
Round 16: Repeat Round 12.
Round 18: P1, knot, p2, YO, SSK, p2, T1/1/1B, k-tbl, k1, k-tbl, T1/1/1F, p2, k2tog, YO, p2, knot, p1.
Round 20: P1, [k2, p2] 2x, k2tog, YO, p2, k-tbl, p1, YO, SSK, k1, k2tog, YO, p1, k-tbl, p2, YO, SSK, [p2, k2] 2x, p1.

Work in pattern until leg measures approximately 6" from start (or desired length to top of heel flap), ending with *Back Leg Pattern* Round 7.

Heel Flap

Work across instep stitches in pattern. The heel flap will now be worked back-and-forth over the 35 heel stitches as follows (or from chart on p. 20):
Row 1 (RS): Sl1, knot, p2, k2tog, YO, p2, T1/1/1B, k-tbl, k1, k-tbl, T1/1/1F, p2, YO, SSK, p2, knot, k1.
Row 2 (and all WS rows through Row 20): Sl1, [p2, k2] 3x, p1, k1, p5, k1, p1, [k2, p2] 2x, k2, p3.

Row 3: Sl1, [k2, p2] 2x, YO, SSK, p2, k-tbl, p1, YO, SSK, k1, k2tog, YO, p1, k-tbl, p2, k2tog, YO, p2, k2, p2, k3.
Row 5: Sl1, [k2, p2] 2x, k2tog, YO, p2, k-tbl, p1, k-tbl, YO, SK2P, YO, k-tbl, p1, k-tbl, p2, YO, SSK, p2, k2, p2, k3.
Row 7: Sl1, [k2, p2] 2x, YO, SSK, p2, k-tbl, p1, k-tbl, YO, SK2P, YO, k-tbl, p1, k-tbl, p2, k2tog, YO, p2, k2, p2, k3.
Row 9: Repeat Row 5.
Row 11: Sl1, knot, p2, YO, SSK, p2, T1/1/1B, k-tbl, k1, k-tbl, T1/1/1F, p2, k2tog, YO, p2, knot, k1.
Row 13: Sl1, [k2, p2] 2x, k2tog, YO, p2, k-tbl, p1, YO, SSK, k1, k2tog, YO, p1, k-tbl, p2, YO, SSK, p2, k2, p2, k3.
Row 15: Sl1, [k2, p2] 2x, YO, SSK, p2, k-tbl, p1, k-tbl, YO, SK2P, YO, k-tbl, p1, k-tbl, p2, k2tog, YO, p2, k2, p2, k3.
Row 17: Sl1, [k2, p2] 2x, k2tog, YO, p2, k-tbl, p1, k-tbl, YO, SK2P, YO, k-tbl, p1, k-tbl, p2, YO, SSK, p2, k2, p2, k3.
Row 19: Repeat Row 15.
Work Rows 1-20, then repeat Rows 1-14 once more for a total of 34 heel flap rows.

Turn Heel

Row 1 (RS): Sl1, k17, SSK, k1, turn.
Row 2: Sl1, p2, p2tog, p1, turn.
Row 3: Sl1, knit to stitch before gap formed by previous row's turn, SSK, k1, turn.

Row 4: Sl1, purl to stitch before gap formed by previous row's turn, p2tog, p1, turn.

Repeat Rows 3-4 until all heel flap stitches have been worked. 19 heel stitches remain.

Shape Gusset

Knit across the 19 heel stitches. Working up the side of the heel flap with the same needle, pu 17 stitches. Work instep stitches in pattern as established. Working down the other side of the heel flap with an empty dpn or empty end of second circular needle, pu 17 stitches. 53 heel stitches.

If using dpns, knit the first 10 stitches from the second heel needle onto the first so there are approximately an equal number of heel stitches on each needle.

To get back to the beginning of the round, knit to the end of the heel stitches.

Round 1: Work instep stitches in pattern as established; knit to last 3 heel stitches, k2tog, k1.

Round 2: Work instep stitches in pattern as established; k1, SSK, knit to end of heel stitches. 51 heel stitches.

Repeat Rounds 1-2 an additional 8x, then work Round 1 once more. 34 heel stitches, 68 total stitches.

Foot

Continue to work instep stitches in pattern as established and heel stitches in stockinette stitch until foot from start of heel turn to needles measures approximately 2" less than desired finished bottom-of-foot length.

Toe

Round 1: Knit.

Round 2: *K1, SSK, knit to last 3 instep stitches, k2tog, k1; repeat from * across heel stitches. 64 stitches.

Repeat Rounds 1-2 an additional 9x. 28 stitches. Then, repeat Round 2 only an additional 3x. 16 stitches.

Cut yarn, leaving a 14-16" tail. Graft toe closed using Kitchener Stitch.

Finishing

Weave in any remaining ends, dampen socks and lay flat to block or use sock blockers.

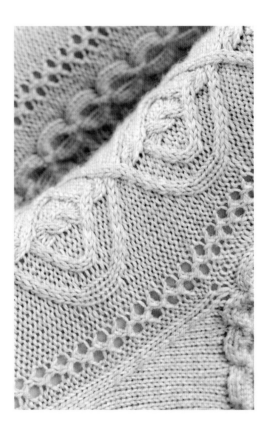

Instep Ribbing

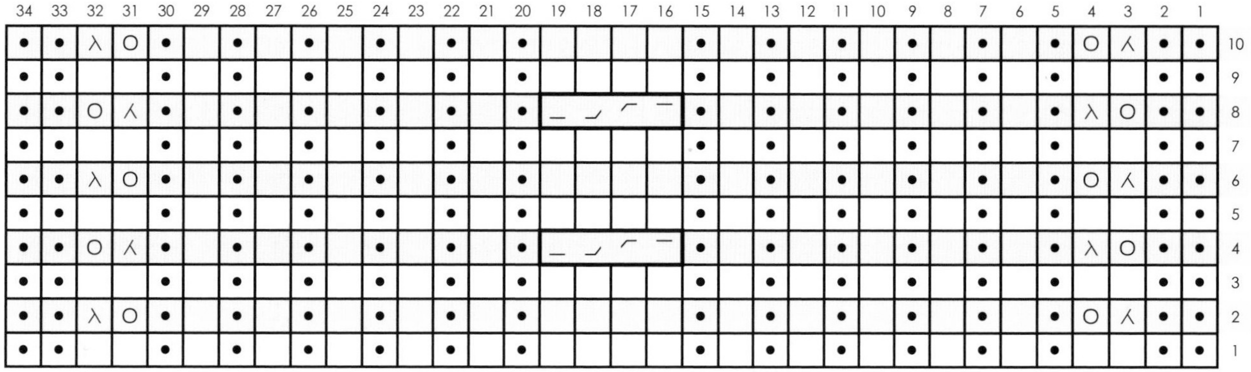
34 33 32 31 30 29 28 27 26 25 24 23 22 21 20 19 18 17 16 15 14 13 12 11 10 9 8 7 6 5 4 3 2 1
10 9 8 7 6 5 4 3 2 1

Back Leg Ribbing

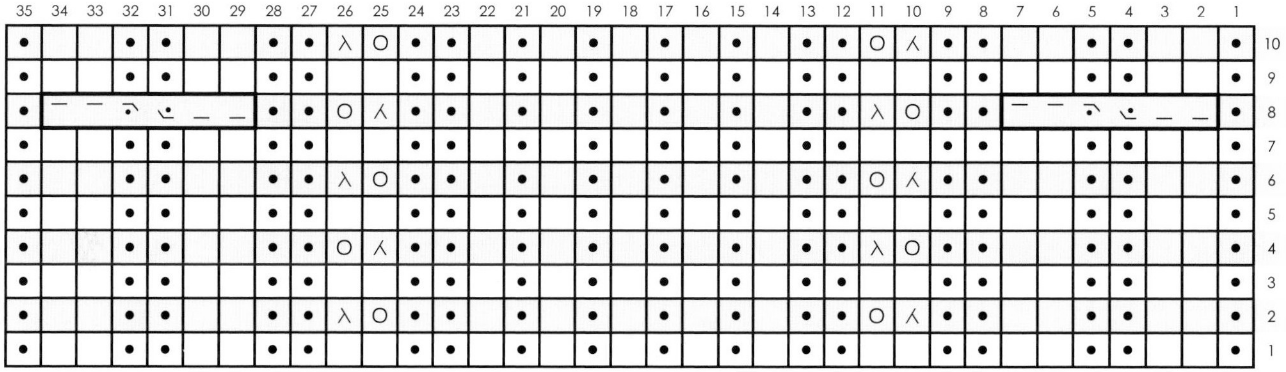
35 34 33 32 31 30 29 28 27 26 25 24 23 22 21 20 19 18 17 16 15 14 13 12 11 10 9 8 7 6 5 4 3 2 1
10 9 8 7 6 5 4 3 2 1

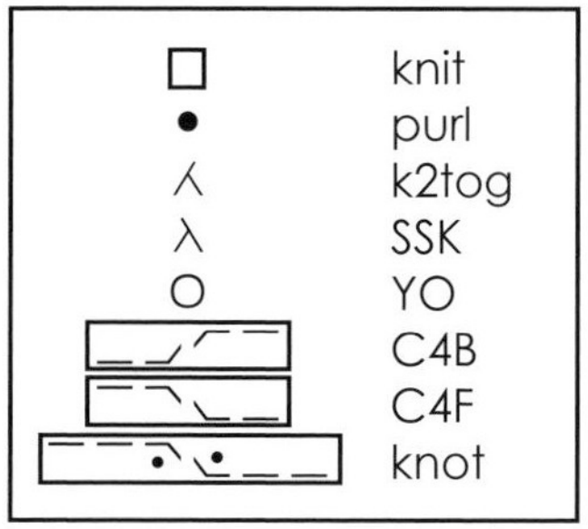
knit
purl
k2tog
SSK
YO
C4B
C4F
knot

Instep Cable Pattern

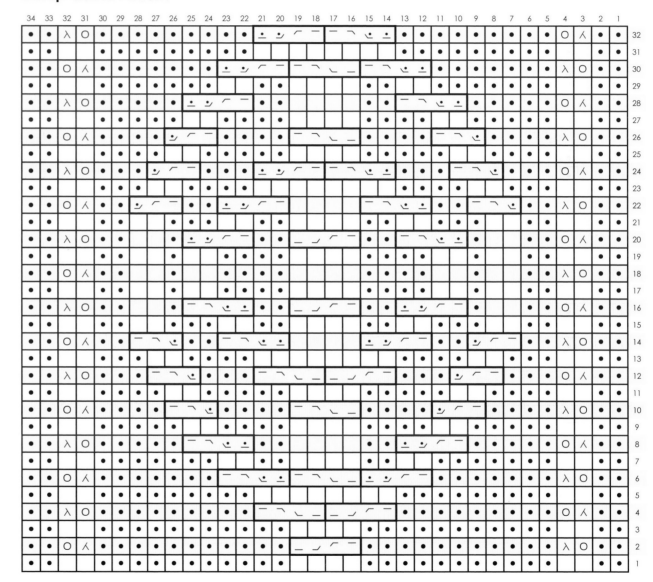

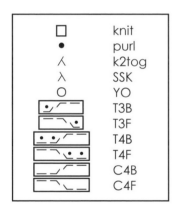

□	knit
•	purl
人	k2tog
λ	SSK
○	YO
T3B	T3B
T3F	T3F
T4B	T4B
T4F	T4F
C4B	C4B
C4F	C4F

Back Leg Pattern

Columns (top): 35 34 33 32 31 30 29 28 27 26 25 24 23 22 21 20 19 18 17 16 15 14 13 12 11 10 9 8 7 6 5 4 3 2 1

Rows (right side): 20 19 18 17 16 15 14 13 12 11 10 9 8 7 6 5 4 3 2 1

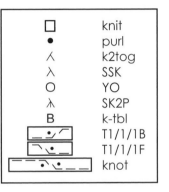

Symbol	Meaning
□	knit
•	purl
人	k2tog
λ	SSK
O	YO
人	SK2P
B	k-tbl
	T1/1/1B
	T1/1/1F
	knot

Heel Flap Pattern

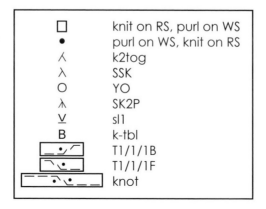

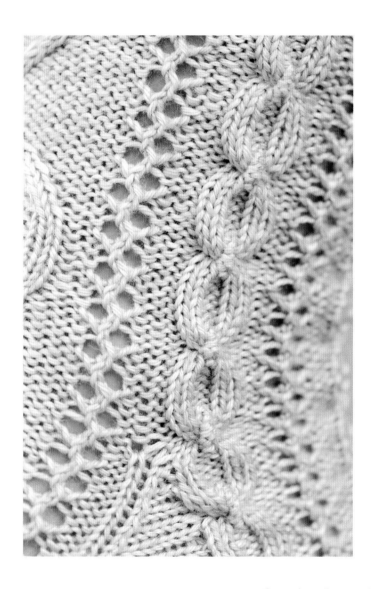

Shalimar Yarns

Hand Paint Original

Materials:

Approximately 400 yards of fingering-weight yarn. *Sample uses Shalimar Yarns Zoe Sock (100% superwash merino wool) in 'Sprout'.*

US1 (2.25mm) needles or size needed to obtain gauge

Yarn needle

Gauge:

9 stitches/12 rounds per inch in stockinette stitch

Size:

Foot circumference = approximately 7-1/2"

Sprout Socks

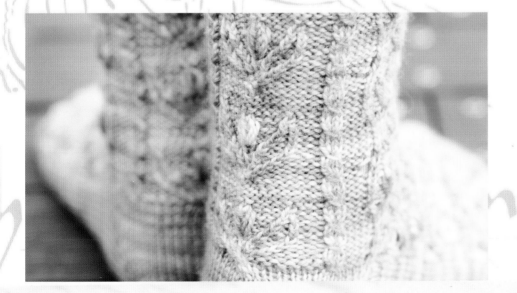

Designer's Notes:

The subtle shades of green in this colorway are delightful, both in the skein and knit up into these fun socks, which were inspired by the yarn's colorway name, *Sprout*.

Lighter semi-solids like this one allow for quite a bit of play, so I found a fun stitch reminiscent of bean sprouts to run up the front of the sock, paired with some small seedlings for the back.

Long loops and slip-stitch mock cables are two elements that could work very well with a busier variegated yarn, although the seedlings on the back may get lost in the shuffle. Feel free to experiment - take the bean sprout motif, pair it with a intensely variegated green yarn, and extend it around the leg for a fun explosion of color.

No matter which yarn decides it wants to be made into Sprout Socks, they're sure to be a hit with the garden-lover in your life.

Special Abbreviations and Techniques for This Pattern

C5B-tbl: Sl3 to cable needle and hold in back, k-tbl 2x, k-tbl 3x from cable needle

long loop: Insert needle from front to back into stitch 4 rows below next stitch and pull up a loop. Bring yarn to front of work. Insert needle from back to front in same stitch and pull up another loop. Bring yarn to back of work. Insert needle from front to back in same stitch and pull up a third loop. Drop next stitch off left needle - it will ladder down to stitch where long loops originate.

sl-left: Sl3, pass 3rd stitch on right needle over first two stitches and off the needle, slip those same two stitches back to the left needle, k1, YO, k1.

T2B-tbl: Sl1 to cable needle and hold in back, k1-tbl, p1 from cable needle.

T2F-tbl: Sl1 to cable needle and hold in front, p1, k1-tbl from cable needle.

Toe

Using Judy's Magic Cast-On (or your favorite toe-up cast on), cast on 9 instep stitches and 9 heel stitches (18 total stitches), dividing them over your selected needles.

Round 1: Knit.

Round 2: *K-fb, knit to last 2 instep stitches, k-fb, k1; repeat from * across heel stitches. 22 stitches.
Repeat Round 2 only an additional 2x. 30 stitches. Then, repeat Rounds 1-2 an additional 9x. 66 stitches, 33 instep and 33 heel.

Foot

Begin working *Instep Pattern* as follows (or from chart on p. 26) across the instep stitches. Continue working heel stitches in stockinette stitch.

Instep Pattern

(over 33 stitches and 16 rounds)
Round 1: P3, [k3, p5] 3x, k3, p3.
Round 2: P2, [k2tog, YO, p1, YO, SSK, p3] 3x, k2tog, YO, p1, YO, SSK, p2.
Round 3: P2, [k1, p3] 7x, k1, p2.
Round 4: [P1, k2tog, YO, p3, YO, SSK] 4x, p1.
Round 5: K2, [p5, k3] 3x, p5, k2.
Round 6: K2, [p2, long loop, p2, k3] 3x, p2, long loop, p2, k2. 41 stitches.
Round 7: K2, [p2, k3] 7x, p2, k2.
Round 8: K2, [p2, S2KP, p2, k3] 3x, p2, S2KP, p2, k2. 33 stitches.
Round 9: K2, [p5, k3] 3x, p5, k2.
Round 10: [P1, YO, SSK, p3, k2tog, YO] 4x, p1.
Round 11: P2, [k1, p3] 7x, k1, p2.
Round 12: P2, [YO, SSK, p1, k2tog, YO, p3] 3x, YO, SSK, p1, k2tog, YO, p2.
Round 13: P3, [k3, p5] 3x, k3, p3.
Round 14: [Long loop, p2, k3, p2, long loop. 43 stitches.
Round 15: [K3, p2] 8x, k3.
Round 16: [S2KP, p2, k3, p2] 4x, S2KP. 33 stitches.
Repeat Rounds 1-16 until foot measures approximately 2" less than desired finished foot length.

Heel

Work across instep stitches in pattern. The heel turn will now be worked back-and-forth over the 33 heel stitches.

Shape Bottom of Heel

Row 1 (RS): K32, W&T.
Row 2 (WS): P31, W&T.
Row 3: Knit to stitch before wrapped stitch (do not knit any wrapped stitches), W&T.
Row 4: Purl to stitch before wrapped stitch (do not purl any wrapped stitches), W&T.
Repeat Rows 3-4 an additional 9x – there are now 11 wrapped stitches on either side of 11 unwrapped center stitches.

Shape Top of Heel

Row 1 (RS): Knit to first wrapped stitch (do not knit across any wrapped stitches), lift wrap RS, turn.
Row 2 (WS): Purl to first wrapped stitch (do not purl across any wrapped stitches), lift wrap WS, turn.

Row 3: Sl1, knit to next wrapped stitch (just past the stitch unwrapped on the previous RS row), lift wrap RS, turn.

Row 4: Sl1, purl to next wrapped stitch (just past the stitch unwrapped on the previous WS row), lift wrap WS, turn.

Repeat Rows 3-4 an additional 8x – a single wrapped stitch remains on either side of heel.

Next Row: Sl1, knit to last wrapped stitch, lift wrap RS but do not turn. You should be at the beginning of the instep stitches.

Next Round: Work instep stitches in next round of *Instep Pattern*; lift wrap RS, knit to end of heel stitches.

Leg

Continue to work the instep stitches in *Instep Pattern* as established. Begin working the heel stitches in *Back Leg Pattern* as follows (or from chart on p. 27) across all stitches. Begin *Back Leg Pattern* on same round as *Instep Pattern* so that the design will line up around the leg.

Back Leg Pattern

(over 33 stitches and 16 rounds)

Round 1: P2, k1, p3, k3, p15, k3, p3, k1, p2.

Round 2: P1, k2tog, YO, p3, sl-left, p5, C5B-tbl, p5, sl-left, p3, YO, SSK, p1.

Round 3: P1, k1, p4, k3, p5, k-tbl 5x, p5, k3, p4, k1, p1.

Round 4: K2tog, YO, p4, k3, p4, T2B-tbl, k-tbl 3x, T2F-tbl, p4, k3, p4, YO, SSK.

Round 5: K1, p5, k3, p3, T2B-tbl, p1, k-tbl 3x, p1, T2F-tbl, p3, k3, p5, k1.

Round 6: K1, p5, sl-left, p2, T2B-tbl, p1, T2B-tbl, k1, T2F-tbl, p1, T2F-tbl, p2, sl-left, p5, k1.

Round 7: K1, p5, k3, [p2, k-tbl] 2x, p1, k1, p1, [k-tbl, p2] 2x, k3, p5, k1.

Round 8: K1, p5, k3, p2, k-tbl, p1, T2B-tbl, p1, k1, p1, T2F-tbl, p1, k-tbl, p2, k3, p5, k1.

Round 9: K1, p5, k3, p2, k-tbl, p1, k-tbl, p2, k1, p2, k-tbl, p1, k-tbl, p2, k3, p5, k1.

Round 10: YO, SSK, p4, sl-left, p2, k-tbl, T2B-tbl, p2, long loop, p2, T2F-tbl, k-tbl, p2, sl-left, p4, k2tog, YO. 35 stitches.

Round 11: P1, k1, p4, k3, p2, k-tbl 2x, p3, k3, p3, k-tbl 2x, p2, k3, p4, k1, p1.

Round 12: P1, YO, SSK, p3, k3, p2, T2B-tbl, p3, S2KP, p3, T2F-tbl, p2, k3, p3, k2tog, YO, p1.

Round 13: Repeat Round 1.

Round 14: P2, k1, p3, sl-left, p15, sl-left, p3, k1, p2.

Rounds 15-16: Repeat Round 1.

Work in pattern until the leg measures approximately 5" from top of heel (or 3/4" less than desired finished length).

Cuff

Work cuff in ribbing pattern as follows:

Round 1: *P1, k1; repeat from * to end of round.

Repeat Round 1 an additional 6x.

Bind off all stitches loosely as follows: K1, *YO, k1, using tip of left needle, pass 2nd and 3rd stitches on right needle over 1st stitch on right needle (one stitch remains on right needle); repeat from * until all stitches are bound off. Fasten off.

Finishing

Weave in any remaining ends, dampen socks and lay flat to block or use sock blockers.

Instep Pattern

Legend:

- □ knit
- k3 k3
- • purl
- ○ YO
- λ SSK
- ⅄ k2tog
- Λ S2KP
- (long loop symbol) long loop

Column numbers (left to right): 33 32 31 30 29 28 27 26 25 24 23 22 21 20 19 18 17 16 15 14 13 12 11 10 9 8 7 6 5 4 3 2 1

Row numbers (bottom to top): 1 – 16

Back Leg Pattern

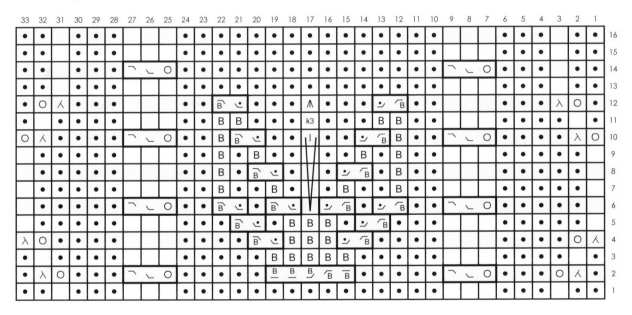

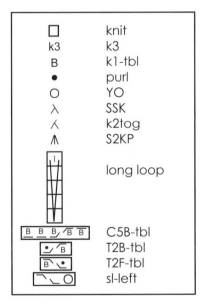

knit
k3 → k3
B → k1-tbl
• → purl
O → YO
λ → SSK
ʎ → k2tog
Λ → S2KP
long loop
C5B-tbl
T2B-tbl
T2F-tbl
sl-left

Curious Creek
FIBERS

Materials:

Approximately 350 (425, 475) yards of dk-weight yarn, more for a particularly long foot or wide/long calf. *Sample uses Curious Creek Serengeti (100% superwash merino wool) in 'Old Head of Kinsale' (adult socks) and 'Sunrise on Daffodils' (child's socks).*

US2 (2.5mm) needles or size needed to obtain gauge

Yarn needle

Gauge:

7 stitches/9 rounds per inch in stockinette stitch

Size:

Foot circumference = approximately 6-1/2 (8, 9-1/2)"

Ulmaceae Lane

Designer's Notes:

Kristine, the mastermind behind Curious Creek's pleasing, subtle colorways, requested that I design some fun knee-highs with the yarn she sent. She offered up a dk-weight to make the prospect of all that knitting slightly less daunting.

I opted to combine a diamond-shaped leaf motif with a slip-stitch mock cable on the front and calf-hugging ribbing down the back of the leg. A reverse-stockinette sole allows for a different look at the yarn as well as placing the smooth stockinette fabric against the bottom of the foot for extra comfort.

For an extra-smooth sole, you might choose to knit the toe and heel in reverse stockinette as well, but I opted for regular stockinette on this sock for design interest and ease of knitting. This fun, unfussy pattern (named after the noble Elm tree) will fly off your needles and onto your legs in no time!

This was the December 2010 Indie Socks CSK featured pattern.

Toe

Using Judy's Magic Cast-On or your favorite toe-up cast on, cast on 5 (7, 9) instep stitches and 5 (7, 9) heel stitches (10, 14, 18 total stitches), dividing them over your selected needles.

Round 1: Knit.
Round 2: *K-fb, knit to last 2 instep stitches, k-fb, k1; repeat from * across heel stitches. 14 (18, 22) stitches.
Repeat Round 2 only an additional 2 (3, 3)x. 22 (30, 34) stitches. Then, repeat Rounds 1-2 an additional 6 (7, 8)x. 46 (58, 66), stitches, 23 (29, 33) instep and 23 (29, 33) heel. Knit one round even.

Foot

Begin working instep stitches in the following order: *Side Pattern A, Instep Center, Side Pattern B* as follows (or from charts on p. 32), separating each section with stitch markers if desired. At same time, begin working heel stitches in reverse stockinette stitch (purl all stitches).

Work until foot measures 1-1/2 (2, 2-1/2)" less than desired finished length from tip of toe, ending with Round 1, 5, 9 or 13 of *Instep Center* pattern.

Note: If the transition between the stockinette toe and reverse stockinette sole bothers your feet (or your sense of aesthetics), feel free to knit the heel/sole stitches in stockinette instead.*

Stitch Patterns

Side Pattern A (6-1/2" size only)
(over 6 stitches and 4 rounds)
Round 1: P1, sl-right, p2.
Rounds 2-4: P1, k3, p2.

Side Pattern A (8" size only)
(over 9 stitches and 4 rounds)
Round 1: [P1, sl-right] 2x, p1.
Rounds 2-4: [P1, k3] 2x, p1.

Side Pattern A (9-1/2" size only)
(over 11 stitches and 4 rounds)
Round 1: P1, [sl-right, p2] 2x.
Rounds 2-4: P1, [k3, p2] 2x.

Instep Center (all sizes)
(over 11 stitches and 16 rounds)
Round 1: SSK, k3, YO, k1, YO, k3, k2tog.
Rounds 2, 4, 6, 8, 10, 12, 14 & 16: K11.
Round 3: SSK, k2, YO, k3, YO, k2, k2tog.
Round 5: SSK, k1, YO, k5, YO, k1, k2tog.
Round 7: SSK, YO, k7, YO, k2tog.
Round 9: K1, YO, k3, SK2P, k3, YO, k1.
Round 11: K2, YO, k2, SK2P, k2, YO, k2.
Round 13: K3, YO, k1, SK2P, k1, YO, k3.
Round 15: K4, YO, SK2P, YO, k4.

Side Pattern B (6-1/2" size only)
(over 6 stitches and 4 rounds)
Round 1: P2, sl-left, p1.
Rounds 2-4: P2, k3, p1.

Side Pattern B (8" size only)
(over 9 stitches and 4 rounds)
Round 1: [P1, sl-left] 2x, p1.
Rounds 2-4: [P1, k3] 2x, p1.

Side Pattern B (9-1/2" size only)
(over 11 stitches and 4 rounds)
Round 1: [P2, sl-left] 2x, p1.
Rounds 2-4: [P2, k3] 2x, p1.

Back Center (all sizes)
(over 11 stitches and 1 round)
Round 1: K2, p2, k3, p2, k2.

Heel

Work across instep stitches in pattern. The heel turn will now be worked back-and-forth over the 23 (29, 33) heel stitches.

Shape Bottom of Heel
Row 1 (RS): K22 (28, 32), W&T.
Row 2 (WS): P21 (27, 31), W&T.
Row 3: Knit to stitch before wrapped stitch (do not knit any wrapped stitches), W&T.
Row 4: Purl to stitch before wrapped stitch (do not purl any wrapped stitches), W&T.
Repeat Rows 3-4 an additional 6 (8, 9)x – there are now 8 (10, 11) wrapped stitches on either side of 7 (9, 11) unwrapped center stitches.

Shape Top of Heel

Row 1 (RS): Knit to first wrapped stitch (do not knit across any wrapped stitches), lift wrap RS, turn.

Row 2 (WS): Purl to first wrapped stitch (do not purl across any wrapped stitches), lift wrap WS, turn.

Row 3: Sl1, knit to next wrapped stitch (just past the stitch unwrapped on the previous RS row), lift wrap RS, turn.

Row 4: Sl1, purl to next wrapped stitch (just past the stitch unwrapped on the previous WS row), lift wrap WS, turn.

Repeat Rows 3-4 an additional 5 (7, 8)x – a single wrapped stitch remains on either side of heel.

Next Row: Sl1, knit to last wrapped stitch, lift wrap RS but do not turn. You should be at the beginning of the instep stitches.

Next Round: Work instep stitches in pattern as established; lift wrap RS, knit to end of heel stitches.

Leg

To get a custom-fitted calf shape, measure the circumference of the sock recipient's calf at the widest point. Then, use **Table 1** on p. 33 to determine the optimal number of calf stitches.

The calculations in **Table 1** use approximately 25-30% negative ease which I've found strikes a reasonable balance between a sock leg that's too tight and one that's constantly falling down.

The increase section of the leg should cover approximately the center 1/3. Determine the desired finished length of the leg by measuring from the crease at the back of the knee to the bottom of the ankle bone. Unless your leg is very straight, you will want to add 1/2" - 1" to accomodate the stretch of the fabric over the calf.

Determine where to start the increases using the figures in **Table 2** on p. 33. If your leg length falls outside this table, divide it by three to determine your starting height.

Continue to work the instep stitches in pattern as established. Begin working the heel stitches in the following order: *Side Pattern B, Back Center, Side Pattern A* (from written directions on p. 30 or charts on p. 32-33). Work even in pattern until leg measures the correct 'start increases at' length (from Table 2) from top of heel.

Side Pattern B
(6-1/2" size)

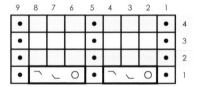

Side Pattern B
(8" size)

Instep Center

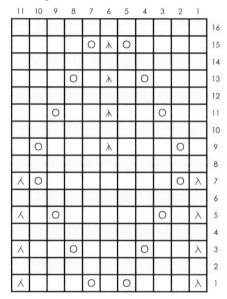

Side Pattern A
(6-1/2" size)

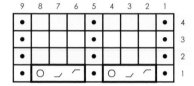

Side Pattern A
(8" size)

Side Pattern B
(9-1/2" size)

Side Pattern A
(9 -1/2" size)

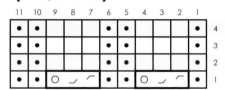

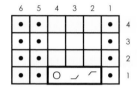

□	knit
●	purl
O	YO
λ	SSK
人	k2tog
木	SK2P
O ⌣	sl-right
⌣ O	sl-left

Table 1:

Calf Circumference:	*10"*	*12"*	*14"*	*16"*	*18"*	*20"*	*22"*	*24"*
# of increases for 6-1/2" Size:	6	10	22	34	42	54	62	70
# of increases for 8" Size:	0	0	10	22	30	42	50	58
# of increases for 9-1/2" Size:	0	0	0	14	22	34	42	54

Table 2:

Leg Length:	*12"*	*13"*	*14"*	*15"*	*16"*	*17"*	*18"*	*19"*
Start increases ___" from top of heel:	4"	4-1/4"	4-3/4"	5"	5-1/4"	5-3/4"	6"	6-1/4"

Back Center

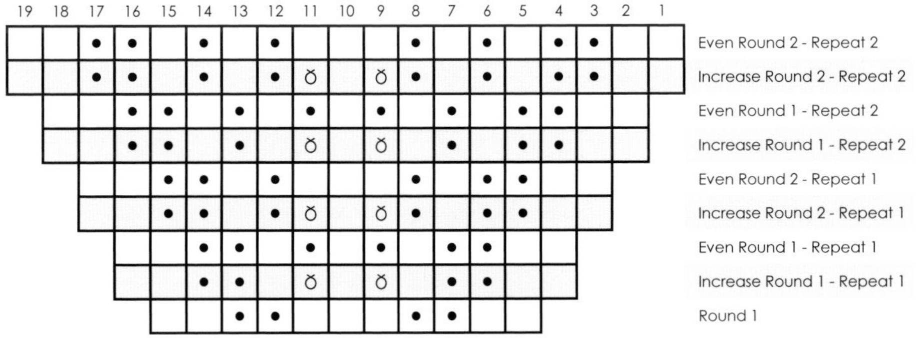
19 18 17 16 15 14 13 12 11 10 9 8 7 6 5 4 3 2 1
Even Round 2 - Repeat 2
Increase Round 2 - Repeat 2
Even Round 1 - Repeat 2
Increase Round 1 - Repeat 2
Even Round 2 - Repeat 1
Increase Round 2 - Repeat 1
Even Round 1 - Repeat 1
Increase Round 1 - Repeat 1
Round 1

□ knit
• purl
ŏ m1

Note: This chart is not complete, but is a visual to get you started on your increases. Be sure to read line-by-line instructions on p.34 for complete details on how to work the calf shaping.

Increase Section

Work a round in pattern, placing a stitch marker after the 12th (15th, 17th) heel stitch to mark the center back of the leg.

Increase Round 1: Work across instep stitches in pattern; work across heel stitches in pattern to stitch before marker, m1, k1 || m1, work to end of round. Two stitches increased.

Even Round 1 (if working fewer than 34 increases, work this round 3x; if working 34+ increases, work this round once): Work across instep stitches in pattern; work across heel stitches in pattern to 2 stitches before marker, p1, k1 || p1, work to end of round.

Increase Round 2: Repeat Increase Round 1.

Even Round 2 (if working fewer than 34 increases, work this round 3x; if working 34+ increases, work this round once): Work across instep stitches in pattern; work across heel stitches in pattern to 2 stitches before marker, k2 || k1, work to end of round.

Repeat Increase Rounds 1-2 and accompanying Even Rounds until correct number of stitches needed for your size has been increased, ending with Increase Round 1.

Work even in pattern as established until leg measures 2 (2-1/4, 2-1/2)" less than desired finished length, ending with an even-numbered pattern round. Do not remove marker at center back of leg.

Decrease Section

Decrease Round 1: Work across instep stitches in pattern; work across heel stitches in pattern to two stitches before marker, S2KP (move marker just to left of decrease), work to end of round. Two stitches decreased.

Next Round: Work across instep stitches in pattern; work across heel stitches in pattern as established.
Repeat last two rounds once more. Four stitches decreased.

Cuff

Work cuff in ribbing pattern as follows:
Round 1 (6-1/2" size only): P1, k3, p2, k2, p2, k3, p2, k2, p2, k3, p1; p1, k3, p2, k2, p2, [k1, p1] to 2 stitches before center marker, k2 || k1, [p1, k1] to last 10 stitches, p2, k2, p2, k3, p1.
Round 1 (8" size only): [P1, k3] 2x, p1, k2, p2, k3, p2, k2, p1, [k3, p1] 2x; [p1, k3] 2x, p1, k2, p2, [k1, p1] to 2 stitches before center marker, k2 || k1, [p1, k1] to last 13 stitches, p2, k2, p1, [k3, p1] 2x.

Round 1 (9-1/2" size only): P1, [k3, p2] 2x, k2, p2, k3, p2, k2, [p2, k3] 2x, p1; p1, [k3, p2] 2x, k2, p2, [k1, p1] to 2 stitches before center marker, k2 || k1, [p1, k1] to last 15 stitches, p2, k2, [p2, k3] twice, p1.
Repeat Round 1 an additional 7 (9, 11)x.

Bind off all stitches loosely as follows: K1, *YO, k1, using tip of left needle, pass 2nd and 3rd stitches on right needle over 1st stitch on right needle (one stitch remains on right needle); repeat from * until all stitches are bound off. Fasten off.

Finishing

Weave in any remaining ends, dampen socks and lay flat to block or use sock blockers.

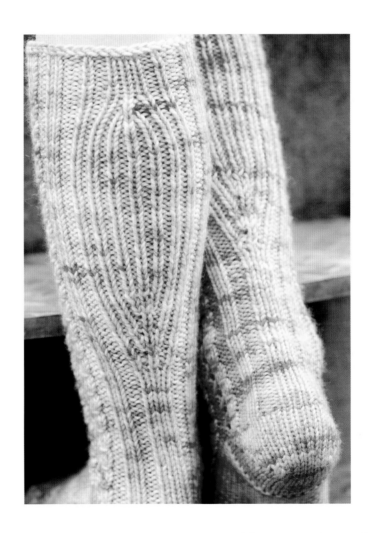

Love Rocks!

The Sweet Sheep
Hand dyed with love
www.thesweetsheep.com

Materials:

Approximately 400 yards of fingering-weight yarn. *Sample uses The Sweet Sheep Sweet Socks Tight Twist (100% superwash merino wool) in 'Love Rocks'.*

US1 (2.25mm) needles or size needed to obtain gauge

Yarn needle

Gauge:

8 stitches/11 rounds per inch in stockinette stitch

Size:

Foot circumference = approximately 7-1/2"

True Love

Designer's Notes:

February is one of my favorite months, as it includes both Valentine's Day and my darling daughter Sydney's birthday.

Sydney is a sporty tomboy with a girlie-girl center, as demonstrated by her love of anything pink and frilly, preferably adorned with kittens, hearts, butterflies and/or unicorns. Assuming she's not on her way to soccer practice, of course!

As soon as I laid eyes on this Love Rocks yarn from The Sweet Sheep, I knew it would be February's yarn. In honor of Sydney and St. Valentine, I found an engaging heart-like cable motif to run up the front of the sock and complete the theme.

A simple twisted rib on the back of the leg gives your eyes, mind and fingers a rest while knitting and helps hug the ankle when worn. They're the perfect Valentine's Day gift - for yourself!

This was the February 2011 Indie Socks CSK featured pattern.

Toe

Using Judy's Magic Cast-On or your favorite toe-up cast on, cast on 8 instep stitches and 8 heel stitches (16 total stitches), dividing them over your selected needles.

Round 1: Knit.
Round 2: *K-fb, knit to last 2 instep stitches, k-fb, k1; repeat from * across heel stitches. 20 stitches.
Repeat Round 2 only an additional 2x. 28 stitches. Then, repeat Rounds 1-2 an additional 11x. 72 stitches, 36 instep and 36 heel. Knit one round even.

Foot

Begin working *Instep Pattern* Rounds 1-20 as follows (or from chart on p. 40) across the instep stitches. Continue working heel stitches in stockinette stitch.

Instep Pattern

(over 36 stitches and 20 rounds)
Round 1: K1, p2, C2F, p2, k2, p7, C4F, p7, k2, p2, C2F, p2, k1.
Round 2: K1, [p2, k2] 2x, p7, k4, p7, [k2, p2] 2x, k1.
Round 3: K1, p2, C2F, p2, k2, p6, T3B, T3F, p6, k2, p2, C2F, p2, k1.
Round 4: K1, [p2, k2] 2x, p6, k2, p2, k2, p6, [k2, p2] 2x, k1.
Round 5: K1, p2, C2F, p2, k2, p5, T3B, p2, T3F, p5, k2, p2, C2F, p2, k1.

Round 6: K1, [p2, k2] 2x, p5, k2, p4, k2, p5, [k2, p2] 2x, k1.
Round 7: K1, p2, C2F, p2, k2, p4, T3B, p4, T3F, p4, k2, p2, C2F, p2, k1.
Round 8: K1, [p2, k2] 2x, p4, k2, p6, k2, p4, [k2, p2] 2x, k1.
Round 9: K1, p2, C2F, p2, k2, p3, T3B 2x, T3F 2x, p3, k2, p2, C2F, p2, k1.
Round 10: K1, [p2, k2] 2x, p3, k2, p1, k2, p2, k2, p1, k2, p3, [k2, p2] 2x, k1.
Round 11: K1, p2, C2F, p2, k2, p2, T3B 2x, p2, T3F 2x, p2, k2, p2, C2F, p2, k1.
Round 12: K1, [p2, k2] 3x, p1, k2, p4, k2, p1, [k2, p2] 3x, k1.
Round 13: K1, p2, C2F, p2, k2, p2, k1, T2F, T3F, p2, T3B, T2B, k1, p2, k2, p2, C2F, p2, k1.
Round 14: K1, [p2, k2] 2x, p2, [k1, p1] 2x, k2, p2, k2, [p1, k1] 2x, p2, [k2, p2] 2x, k1.
Round 15: K1, p2, C2F, p2, k2, p2, k1, p1, T2F, T3F, T3B, T2B, p1, k1, p2, k2, p2, C2F, p2, k1.
Round 16: K1, [p2, k2] 2x, [p2, k1] 2x, p1, k4, p1, [k1, p2] 2x, [k2, p2] 2x, k1.
Round 17: K1, p2, C2F, p2, k2, p2, T2F, T2B, p1, C4F, p1, T2F, T2B, p2, k2, p2, C2F, p2, k1.
Round 18: K1, [p2, k2] 2x, p3, C2F, p2, k4, p2, C2B, p3, [k2, p2] 2x, k1.
Round 19: K1, p2, C2F, p2, k2, p7, k4, p7, k2, p2, C2F, p2, k1.
Round 20: K1, [p2, k2] 2x, p7, k4, p7, [k2, p2] 2x, k1.

Repeat Rounds 1-20 until foot measures approximately 5" less than desired finished foot length (you can end on any pattern round).

Gusset

Round 1: Work instep stitches in *Instep Pattern* as established; k-fb in first heel stitch, knit to last 2 heel stitches, k-fb, k1.
Round 2: Work instep stitches in *Instep Pattern* as established; knit across all heel stitches.
Repeat Rounds 1-2 an additional 16x, then work Round 1 once more. 72 heel stitches.

Turn Heel

Work across instep stitches in pattern. The heel turn will be worked back-and-forth over the 72 heel stitches.
Row 1 (RS): K53, W&T.
Row 2 (WS): P34, W&T.
Row 3: Knit to stitch before wrapped stitch (do not knit any wrapped stitches), W&T.
Row 4: Purl to stitch before wrapped stitch (do not purl any wrapped stitches), W&T.
Repeat Rows 3-4 an additional 10x – there are now 12 wrapped stitches on either side of 12 unwrapped center stitches.

Knit to end of heel stitches, lifting wraps RS as they are encountered, then work across instep stitches in pattern.

Heel Flap

Work the heel flap back and forth.

Row 1 (RS): K53, lifting remaining wraps RS as you encounter them, SSK, turn.

Row 2 (WS): [Sl1, p1] 17x, sl1, p2tog, turn.

Row 3: Sl1, k34, SSK, turn.

Row 4: Repeat Row 2.

Repeat Rows 3-4 an additional 15x, then work Row 3 once more but do not turn. As you do this, you are slowly working up the edge of the gusset and forming the heel flap as you go. At the end, you are left with 73 stitches, 36 instep and 37 heel.

Next Round: Work across instep stitches in pattern; k2tog, knit to end of heel stitches. 72 stitches, 36 instep and 36 heel.

Leg

Continue to work the instep stitches in pattern as established. Begin working the heel stitches in *Back Leg Rib* Rounds 1-2 as follows across all stitches.

Back Leg Rib

(over 36 stitches and 2 rounds)

Round 1: K1, [p2, k2, p2, C2F] 2x, p2, [C2F, p2, k2, p2] 2x, k1.

Round 2: K1, [p2, k2] 8x, p2, k1.

Work in pattern until the leg measures approximately 4" from top of heel flap (or 1" less than desired finished length), ending with Round 2 of *Instep Pattern*.

Cuff

Work cuff in ribbing pattern as follows (or from charts on p. 40):

Rounds 1-8: K1, [p2, k2] 2x, [p1, k1] 3x, p1, k4, p1, [k1, p1] 3x, [k2, p2] 2x, k1; k1, [p2, k2] 8x, p2, k1.

Bind off all stitches loosely as follows: K1, *YO, k1, using tip of left needle, pass 2nd and 3rd stitch on right needle over 1st stitch on right needle (one stitch remains on right needle); repeat from * until all stitches are bound off. Fasten off.

Finishing

Weave in any remaining ends, dampen socks and lay flat to block or use sock blockers.

Instep Pattern

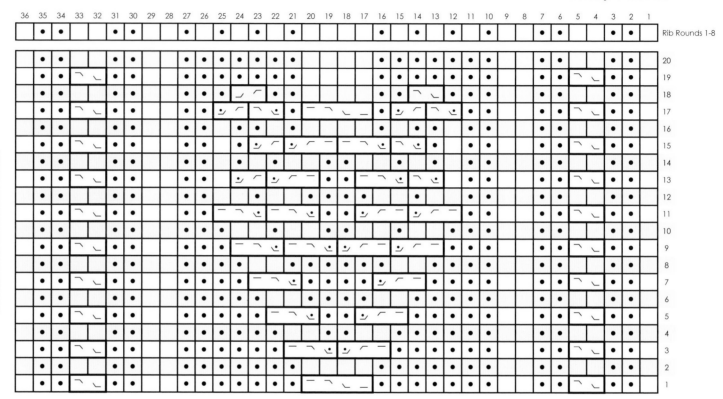

Legend

Symbol	Meaning
□	knit
•	purl
⟍	C2F
⟋	C2B
⟍	C4F
⟍	T2F
⟍	T2B
⟍	T3F
⟍	T3B

Back Leg Pattern

To get a great custom fit, you'll want to measure your (or the sock recipient's) foot carefully. The most important measurement used in most sock patterns is the circumference of the ball of the foot at the widest point (foot circumference).

When knitting a pattern with texture (knit/purl designs), ribbing, or lace, you'll want to choose a sock size that's 10-20% smaller than your actual measurement (or 10-20% negative ease). This will give a fit that hugs your foot nicely and doesn't sag around your ankles.

Make sure to try your sock on frequently as you knit to ensure it's fitting correctly and that the pattern isn't stretched out so much that it's unpleasantly distorted.

For patterns that have less natural stretch to them (this would include twisted stitch patterns, cables or colorwork), you won't want to make the sock much smaller than your actual foot size or it's likely you won't be able to get the sock over your heel. In this situation, you'd want about 5-10% negative ease. Again, the best way to tell if your sock is going to fit is to try it on frequently as you knit.

The second important measurement is foot length. To accurately measure this, stand on a ruler or tape measure with the back of your heel on the 0" mark and see where your longest toe lands.

Since hand-knit socks aren't nearly as stretchy as commercially-produced socks (which generally have some type of elastic spun into the thread), they'll probably be longer than the other socks in your drawer. You don't want to make your knitted socks too short or the heel will pull down under the bottom of your foot. On the flip side, if you knit them too long, you'll end up with a "bubble heel" hanging off the back of your foot.

Tips & Tricks: Fit

Many thanks to ...
Schaefer Yarn !!

This color is Chamomile

SCH...
Hand Painted Luxury Fibers
Nichole
Content: 80% Extrafine Merino Wool
SUPERWASH, 20% Nylon
Approx. Wt: 5 oz./405 yards
Gauge: 7.5 sts/in on US #2

Materials:

Approximately 400 yards of fingering-weight yarn. *Sample uses Schaefer Nichole (80% superwash merino, 20% nylon) in 'Chamomile'.*

US1 (2.25mm) needles or size needed to obtain gauge

Yarn needle, cable needle

Gauge:

8 stitches/12 rounds per inch in stockinette stitch

Size:

Foot circumference = approximately 7"
Note: the lace pattern is quite stretchy, so this should fit feet up to 8-1/2".

Calpurnia

Designer's Notes:

Beware the Ides of March! For the March CSK design, I decided to go all out and design an elegant, complicated sock named after the widow of Julius Caesar.

Knit from the top-down, it begins with a picot edging and moves into a complex, feminine cable-and-lace design down the front of the sock and a floral vine motif down the back of the leg and the heel flap.

I've been waiting to use both of these patterns in a new design and found the squishy Nichole yarn to be the perfect texture and color for this pattern. Calpurnia will tax your brain and put your skills to the test, but when you're done, you will have a pair of stockings truly fit for a queen.

This was the March 2011 Indie Socks CSK featured pattern.

Special Abbreviations and Techniques for This Pattern

bobble: K-fbf, [turn, k3] 3x, turn, slip 2 stitches together as if to knit, k1, pass 2 slipped stitches over first stitch on right needle

C1/2B: Sl2 to cable needle and hold in back, k1, k2 from cable needle

C1/2F: Sl1 to cable needle and hold in front, k2, k1 from cable needle

dec4 (RS): Slip two stitches one at a time as if to knit, *pass 2nd stitch on left needle over 1st stitch, slip stitch to right needle, pass 2nd stitch on right needle over 1st stitch, slip stitch to left needle; repeat from *, k1 (4 stitches decreased)

dec4 (WS): Slip two stitches one at a time as if to purl, *pass 2nd stitch on left needle over 1st stitch, slip stitch to right needle, pass 2nd stitch on right needle over 1st stitch, slip stitch to left needle; repeat from *, p1 (4 stitches decreased)

T1/1/1B: Sl2 to cable needle and hold in back, k1, [p1, k1] from cable needle

T1/1/1F: Sl1 to cable needle and hold in front, k1, p1, k1 from cable needle

T1/2B: Sl2 to cable needle and hold in back, k1, p2 from cable needle

T1/2F: Sl1 to cable needle and hold in front, p2, k1 from cable needle

Cuff

Cast on 62 stitches and divide them over dpns or circular needles as follows:

- If using dpns, place 16 stitches on needles 1 and 2 and 15 stitches on needles 3 and 4.
- If using circular needle(s), place 30 stitches on needle 1 and 32 stitches on needle 2.

The first 32 stitches of the round are the instep stitches and the last 30 stitches are the heel stitches. Join stitches into round being careful not to twist.

Rounds 1-2: Knit.
Round 3: *K2tog, YO; repeat from * to end of round.
Rounds 4-5: Knit.
Round 6: Fold cuff over with WS together so that cast-on edge is behind and even with live stitches on needle, lining edge up so that cast-on stitch is directly behind the live stitch in the same stitch column (this keeps edge flat after hemming). Hem picot edge as follows: *with tip of left needle, pick up cast-on edge stitch, then knit cast-on edge stitch together with live stitch; repeat from * to end of round.
Round 7: Purl.
Round 8: *K2tog, YO; repeat from * to end of round.

Round 9: Purl. Rearrange stitches so that there are 31 instep stitches and 31 heel stitches (if using dpns, there should now be 16 stitches on needles 1 and 3, and 15 stitches on needles 2 and 4; if using circular needle(s), there should be 31 stitches on each needle).
Round 10: *K7, k-fb, k15, k-fb, k7; repeat from *. 66 stitches, 33 instep and 33 heel.

Leg

Begin working *Angel Lace Pattern* across the 33 instep stitches, and *Vine Cable Pattern* across the 33 heel stitches as follows (or from charts on p. 48-49). Work Rounds 1-28 of *Vine Cable Pattern* twice, then work Rounds 1-2 once more.

Angel Lace Pattern

(over 33 stitches and 28 rounds)
Setup Round (work only once at beginning): [P1, k1] 3x, p2, k8, p1, k8, p2, [k1, p1] 3x.
Round 1: P1, T1/1/1F, p1, k1, p2, k3, k2tog, k3, YO, p1, YO, k3, SSK, k3, p2, k1, p1, T1/1/1B, p1.
Round 2: [P1, k1] 3x, p2, k2, k2tog, k3, YO, k1, p1, k1, YO, k3, SSK, k2, p2, [k1, p1] 3x.
Round 3: P1, k1, p1, T1/1/1B, p2, k1, k2tog, k3, YO, k2tog, YO, p1, YO, SSK, YO, k3, SSK, k1, p2, T1/1/1F, p1, k1, p1.

Round 4: [P1, k1] 3x, p2, k2tog, k3, YO, [p1, k2] 2x, p1, YO, k3, SSK, p2, [k1, p1] 3x.

Round 5: P1, T1/1/1F, p1, k1, p2, YO, SSK, k2tog, YO, p2, YO, SSK, p1, k2tog, YO, p2, YO, SSK, k2tog, YO, p2, k1, p1, T1/1/1B, p1.

Round 6: [P1, k1] 3x, p2, k2, p4, k2, p1, k2, p4, k2, p2, [k1, p1] 3x.

Round 7: P1, k1, p1, T1/1/1B, p2, k1, YO, SSK, p3, k2tog, YO, p1, YO, SSK, p3, k2tog, YO, k1, p2, T1/1/1F, p1, k1, p1.

Round 8: [P1, k1] 3x, p2, k3, p3, k2, p1, k2, p3, k3, p2, [k1, p1] 3x.

Round 9: P1, T1/1/1F, p1, k1, p2, k2, YO, SSK, p2, YO, SSK, p1, k2tog, YO, p2, k2tog, YO, k2, p2, k1, p1, T1/1/1B, p1.

Round 10: [P1, k1] 3x, p2, k4, p2, k2, p1, k2, p2, k4, p2, [k1, p1] 3x.

Round 11: P1, k1, p1, T1/1/1B, p2, YO, k3, SSK, p1, k2tog, YO, p1, YO, SSK, p1, k2tog, k3, YO, p2, T1/1/1F, p1, k1, p1.

Round 12: [P1, k1] 3x, p2, k1, YO, k3, SSK, k2, p1, k2, k2tog, k3, YO, k1, p2, [k1, p1] 3x.

Round 13: P1, T1/1/1F, p1, k1, p2, k2, YO, k3, SSK, k1, p1, k1, k2tog, k3, YO, k2, p2, k1, p1, T1/1/1B, p1.

Round 14: [P1, k1] 3x, p2, k3, YO, k3, SSK, p1, k2tog, k3, YO, k3, p2, [k1, p1] 3x.

Round 15: P1, k1, p1, T1/1/1B, p2, YO, k3, SSK, k3, p1, k3, k2tog, k3, YO, p2, T1/1/1F, p1, k1, p1.

Round 16: [P1, k1] 3x, p2, k1, YO, k3, SSK, k2, p1, k2, k2tog, k3, YO, k1, p2, [k1, p1] 3x.

Round 17: P1, T1/1/1F, p1, k1, p2, YO, SSK, YO, k3, SSK, k1, p1, k1, k2tog, k3, YO, k2tog, YO, p2, k1, p1, T1/1/1B, p1.

Round 18: [P1, k1] 3x, p2, k2, p1, YO, k3, SSK, p1, k2tog, k3, YO, p1, k2, p2, [k1, p1] 3x.

Round 19: P1, k1, p1, T1/1/1B, p2, k2tog, YO, p2, YO, SSK, k2tog, YO, p1, YO, SSK, k2tog, YO, p2, YO, SSK, p2, T1/1/1F, p1, k1, p1.

Round 20: [P1, k1] 3x, p2, k2, p4, k2, p1, k2, p4, k2, p2, [k1, p1] 3x.

Round 21: P1, T1/1/1F, p1, k1, p2, YO, SSK, p3, k2tog, YO, k1, p1, k1, YO, SSK, p3, k2tog, YO, p2, k1, p1, T1/1/1B, p1.

Round 22: [P1, k1] 3x, p2, k2, p3, k3, p1, k3, p3, k2, p2, [k1, p1] 3x.

Round 23: P1, k1, p1, T1/1/1B, p2, k2tog, YO, p2, k2tog, YO, k2, p1, k2, YO, SSK, p2, YO, SSK, p2, T1/1/1F, p1, k1, p1.

Round 24: [P1, k1] 3x, p2, k2, p2, k4, p1, k4, p2, k2, p2, [k1, p1] 3x.

Round 25: P1, T1/1/1F, p1, k1, p2, YO, SSK, p1, k2tog, k3, YO, p1, YO, k3, SSK, p1, k2tog, YO, p2, k1, p1, T1/1/1B, p1.

Round 26: [P1, k1] 3x, p2, k2, k2tog, k3, YO, k1, p1, k1, YO, k3, SSK, k2, p2, [k1, p1] 3x.

Round 27: P1, k1, p1, T1/1/1B, p2, k1, k2tog, k3, YO, k2, p1, k2, YO, k3, SSK, k1, p2, T1/1/1F, p1, k1, p1.

Round 28: [P1, k1] 3x, p2, k2tog, k3, YO, k3, p1, k3, YO, k3, SSK, p2, [k1, p1] 3x.

Vine Cable Pattern

(over a multiple of 33 stitches and 28 rounds)

Setup Round (work only once at beginning): P1, k3, p2, k1, p7, k1, p4, k2, p8, k3, p1.

Round 1: P1, C2F, k1, p2, T1/2F, p5, T2F, p1, T4B, p8, k1, C2B, p1.

Round 2: P1, k3, p4, k1, p6, k1, p1, k2, p10, k3, p1.

Round 3: P1, k1, C2B, p4, T1/2F, p4, T4B, p7, m1, k-fbf, m1, p2, C2F, k1, p1. 37 heel stitches.

Round 4: P1, k3, p6, k1, p4, k2, p9, k5, p2, k3, p1.

Round 5: P1, C2F, k1, p6, T1/2F, T4B, p3, bobble, p5, k5, p2, k1, C2B, p1.

Round 6: P1, k3, p8, k3, p5, k1, p5, k5, p2, k3, p1.

Round 7: P1, k1, C2B, p8, C1/2F, p4, T2B, p5, k1, p3, k1, p2, C2F, k1, p1.

Round 8: P1, k3, p8, k3, p4, k1, p6, k1, p3, k1, p2, k3, p1.

Round 9: P1, C2F, k1, p6, T4B, T1/2F, p1, T2B, p6, k5, p2, k1, C2B, p1.

Round 10: P1, k3, p6, k2, p4, k1, p1, k1, p7, k5, p2, k3, p1.

Round 11: P1, k1, C2B, p6, k2, p4, T1/2F, p7, k5, p2, C2F, k1, p1.

Round 12: P1, k3, p6, k2, p6, k1, p7, dec4, p2, k3, p1. 33 heel stitches.

Round 13: P1, C2F, k1, p6, T4F, p4, k1, p7, k1, p2, k1, C2B, p1.

Round 14: P1, k3, p8, k2, p4, k1, p7, k1, p2, k3, p1.

Round 15: P1, k1, C2B, p8, T4F, p1, T2B, p5, T1/2B, p2, C2F, k1, p1.

Round 16: P1, k3, p10, k2, p1, k1, p6, k1, p4, k3, p1.

Round 17: P1, C2F, k1, p2, m1, k-fbf, m1, p7, T4F, p4, T1/2B, p4, k1, C2B, p1. 37 heel stitches.

Round 18: P1, k3, p2, k5, p9, k2, p4, k1, p6, k3, p1.

Round 19: P1, k1, C2B, p2, k5, p5, bobble, p3, T4F, T1/2B, p6, C2F, k1, p1.

Round 20: P1, k3, p2, k5, p5, k1, p5, k3, p8, k3, p1.

Round 21: P1, C2F, k1, p2, k1, p3, k1, p5, T2F, p4, C1/2B, p8, k1, C2B, p1.

Round 22: P1, k3, p2, k1, p3, k1, p6, k1, p4, k3, p8, k3, p1.

Round 23: P1, k1, C2B, p2, k5, p6, T2F, p1, T1/2B, T4F, p6, C2F, k1, p1.

Round 24: P1, k3, p2, k5, p7, k1, p1, k1, p4, k2, p6, k3, p1.

Round 25: P1, C2F, k1, p2, k5, p7, T1/2B, p4, k2, p6, k1, C2B, p1.

Round 26: P1, k3, p2, dec4, p7, k1, p6, k2, p6, k3, p1. 33 heel stitches.

Round 27: P1, k1, C2B, p2, k1, p7, k1, p4, T4B, p6, C2F, k1, p1.

Round 28: P1, k3, p2, k1, p7, k1, p4, k2, p8, k3, p1.

Heel Flap

Work across instep stitches in pattern. The heel flap will then be worked back-and-forth over the 33 heel stitches as follows (or from chart on p. 50):

Row 1 (RS): Sl1, k1, C2B, p4, T1/2F, p4, T4B, p7, m1, k-fbf, m1, p2, C2F, k1, p1. 37 heel stitches.

Row 2 (WS): Sl1, p3, k2, p5, k9, p2, k4, p1, k6, p3, k1.

Row 3: Sl1, C2F, k1, p6, T1/2F, T4B, p3, bobble, p5, k5, p2, k1, C2B, p1.

Row 4: Sl1, p3, k2, p5, k5, p1, k5, p3, k8, p3, k1.

Row 5: Sl1, k1, C2B, p8, C1/2F, p4, T2B, p5, k1, p3, k1, p2, C2F, k1, p1.

Row 6: Sl1, p3, k2, p1, k3, p1, k6, p1, k4, p3, k8, p3, k1.

Row 7: Sl1, C2F, k1, p6, T4B, T1/2F, p1, T2B, p6, k5, p2, k1, C2B, p1.

Row 8: Sl1, p3, k2, p5, k7, p1, k1, p1, k4, p2, k6, p3, k1.

Row 9: Sl1, k1, C2B, p6, k2, p4, T1/2F, p7, k5, p2, C2F, k1, p1.

Row 10: Sl1, p3, k2, dec4, k7, p1, k6, p2, k6, p3, k1. 33 heel stitches.

Row 11: Sl1, C2F, k1, p6, T4F, p4, k1, p7, k1, p2, k1, C2B, p1.

Row 12: Sl1, p3, k2, p1, k7, p1, k4, p2, k8, p3, k1.

Row 13: Sl1, k1, C2B, p8, T4F, p1, T2B, p5, T1/2B, p2, C2F, k1, p1.

Row 14: Sl1, p3, k4, p1, k6, p1, k1, p2, k10, p3, k1.

Row 15: Sl1, C2F, k1, p2, m1, k-fbf, m1, p7, T4F, p4, T1/2B, p4, k1, C2B, p1. 37 heel stitches.

Row 16: Sl1, p3, k6, p1, k4, p2, k9, p5, k2, p3, k1.

Row 17: Sl1, k1, C2B, p2, k5, p5, bobble, p3, T4F, T1/2B, p6, C2F, k1, p1.

Row 18: Sl1, p3, k8, p3, k5, p1, k5, p5, k2, p3, k1.

Row 19: Sl1, C2F, k1, p2, k1, p3, k1, p5, T2F, p4, C1/2B, p8, k1, C2B, p1.

Row 20: Sl1, p3, k8, p3, k4, p1, k6, p1, k3, p1, k2, p3, k1.

Row 21: Sl1, k1, C2B, p2, k5, p6, T2F, p1, T1/2B, T4F, p6, C2F, k1, p1.

Row 22: Sl1, p3, k6, p2, k4, p1, k1, p1, k7, p5, k2, p3, k1.

Row 23: Sl1, C2F, k1, p2, k5, p7, T1/2B, p4, k2, p6, k1, C2B, p1.

Row 24: Sl1, p3, k6, p2, k6, p1, k7, dec4, k2, p3, k1. 33 heel stitches.

Row 25: Sl1, k1, C2B, p2, k1, p7, k1, p4, T4B, p6, C2F, k1, p1.

Row 26: Sl1, p3, k8, p2, k4, p1, k7, p1, k2, p3, k1.

Row 27: Sl1, C2F, k1, p2, T1/2F, p5, T2F, p1, T4B, p8, k1, C2B, p1.

Row 28: Sl1, p3, k10, p2, k1, p1, k6, p1, k4, p3, k1.

Turn Heel

Row 1 (RS): Sl1, k17, SSK, k1, turn.
Row 2: Sl1, p4, p2tog, p1, turn.
Row 3: Sl1, knit to stitch before gap formed by previous row's turn, SSK, k1, turn.
Row 4: Sl1, purl to stitch before gap formed by previous row's turn, p2tog, p1, turn.

Repeat Rows 3-4 until all heel flap stitches have been worked. 19 heel stitches remain.

Shape Gusset

Knit across the 19 heel stitches. Working up the side of the heel flap with the same needle, pu 14 stitches. Work instep stitches in pattern as established. Working down the other side of the heel flap with an empty dpn or empty end of second circular needle, pu 14 stitches. 47 heel stitches.

If using dpns, knit the first 24 stitches from the second heel needle onto the first so there are approximately an equal number of heel stitches on each needle.

To get back to the beginning of the round, knit to the last 3 heel stitches, k2tog, k1. 46 heel stitches.

Round 1: Work instep stitches in pattern as established; k1, SSK, knit to end of heel stitches.

Round 2: Work instep stitches in pattern as established; knit to last 3 heel stitches, k2tog, k1.

Repeat Rounds 1-2 an additional 5x, then work Round 1 once more. 33 heel stitches, 66 total stitches.

Foot

Continue to work instep stitches in pattern as established and heel stitches in stockinette stitch until foot from start of heel turn to needles measures approximately 2" less than desired finished bottom-of-foot length.

Toe

Round 1: *K1, SSK, knit to last 3 instep stitches, k2tog, k1; repeat from * across heel stitches.
Round 2: Knit. 62 stitches.

Repeat Rounds 1-2 an additional 9x. 26 stitches. Then, repeat Round 1 only an additional 2x. 18 stitches.

Cut yarn, leaving a 14-16" tail. Graft toe closed using Kitchener Stitch.

Finishing

Weave in any remaining ends, dampen socks and lay flat to block or use sock blockers.

Angel Lace Pattern

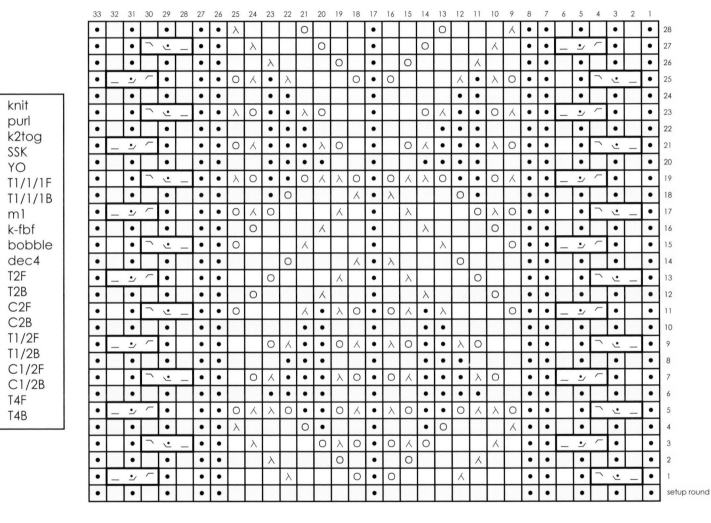

Vine Cable Pattern

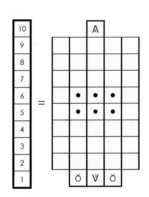

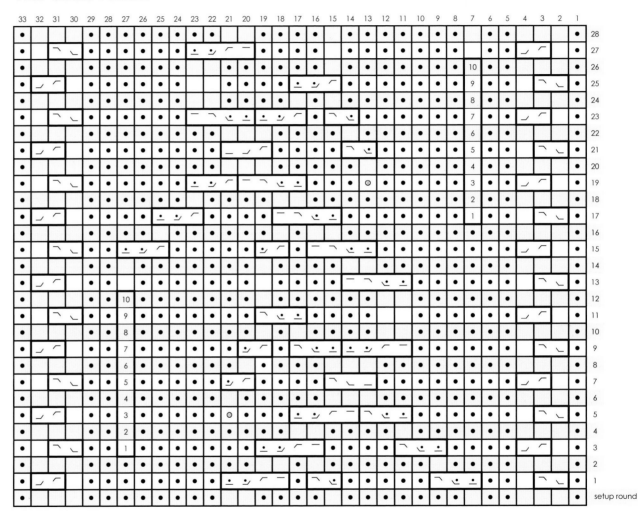

Heel Flap

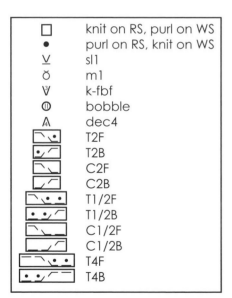

	knit on RS, purl on WS
•	purl on RS, knit on WS
ⱽ	sl1
ŏ	m1
ⱽ	k-fbf
⫿	bobble
⋀	dec4
	T2F
	T2B
	C2F
	C2B
	T1/2F
	T1/2B
	C1/2F
	C1/2B
	T4F
	T4B

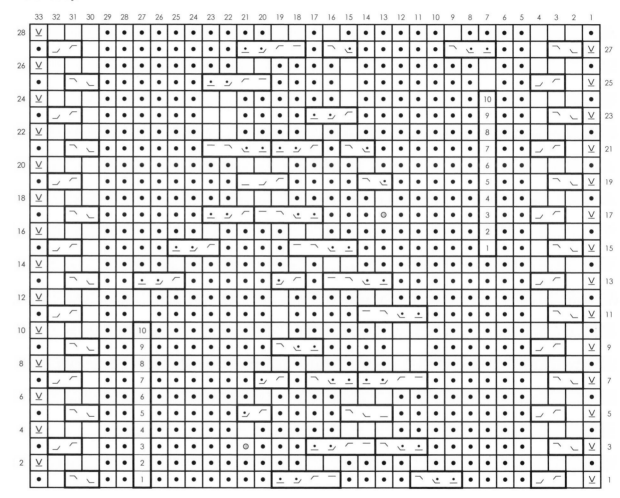

The patterns in this book are written to accommodate the three most common needle methods used for socks: dpns, two circulars and one long circular (aka Magic Loop).

Each pattern gives the needle size in both US number and millimeters, but does not specify type or needle length. Feel free to choose whichever needle type you prefer and start knitting. The patterns refer to "instep stitches" and "heel stitches" instead of numbering the needles. This allows you to divide the stitches according to the needles you're using without confusion.

The instep stitches form the top of the foot and front of the leg. The "heel stitches" include the bottom-of-foot stitches before the heel turn, the stitches used for the heel, and the back-of-leg stitches.

Throughout the book, I refer to dpns and/or circulars. Although it may sound as if I'm excluding the single long circular method entirely, you can instead think of your long needle as two circulars that have a loop of cable in place of two dangling needle tips. The two needle tips of your long circular are the Magic Loop equivalent of two separate needles.

Tips & Tricks: Needle Options

MissBabs:
Hand-dyed
Yarns & Fibers
Mountain City, TN

"Yummy"
Monochrome
Sock & Baby

Yarn - 2 ply

Materials:

Approximately 400 yards of fingering-weight yarn. *Sample uses Miss Babs "Yummy" Monochrome Sock & Baby Yarn (100% merino wool) in 'French Marigold'.*

US1 (2.25mm) needles or size needed to obtain gauge

Yarn needle, cable needle

Gauge:

8 stitches/12 rounds per inch in stockinette stitch

Size:

Foot circumference = approximately 8"

Les Rideaux

Designer's Notes:

Les Rideaux is not the only solid orange sock in this book, but you'll notice that this color is a darker, deeper hue than the fun, bright orange of the Stitch-jones yarn that you'll encounter on p. 70, and seemed to call for a more serious design. While orange is a strong color and not so easily photographed, it does provide a stunning background for complex stitch patterns and cable work.

The design I chose for these socks is reminiscent of theatre curtains, with the front drapes pulled to the side and the back layer hanging straight. I named them with the French words for "the curtains", and found the traveling twisted stitch design engaging and difficult-looking (but not so challenging to actually knit).

Due to the traveling diagonal of the twisted stitches and the purl background, this pattern could work nicely with a busier colorway. You might try swatching with a light- to medium-tone variegated yarn if you don't want to use a solid.

Leg

Cast on 72 stitches and divide them over dpns or circular needles as follows:

- If using dpns, place 20 stitches on needle 1, 18 stitches on needle 2, 18 stitches on needle 3, and 16 stitches on needle 4.
- If using circular needle(s), place 38 stitches on needle 1 and 34 stitches on needle 2.

The first 38 stitches of the round are the instep stitches and the last 34 stitches are the heel stitches. Join stitches into round being careful not to twist.

Begin working *Curtain Pattern* as follows (or from charts on p. 57-58) across all stitches. Work Rounds 1-48 once, then work Rounds 1-23 once more.

Curtain Pattern

(over 72 stitches and 48 rounds)

Round 1: *K2, p3, k3, p4, k3, p3; repeat from * an additional 3x.

Round 2: *YO, SSK, p3, k3, p4, k3, p3, k2tog, YO, p3, k3, p4, k3, p3; repeat from *.

Round 3: Repeat Round 1.

Round 4: *K2tog, YO, p3, sl-left, p4, sl-left, p3, YO, SSK, p3, sl-left, p4, sl-left, p3; repeat from * once more.

Round 5: *K2, p3, k-tbl 3x, p4, k-tbl 3x, p3; repeat from * an additional 3x.

Round 6: *YO, SSK, [p2, T2B, k-tbl, T2F] 2x, p2, k2tog, YO, [p2, T2B, k-tbl, T2F] 2x, p2; repeat from *.

Round 7: *K2, p2, [k-tbl, p1] 2x, k-tbl, p2, [k-tbl, p1] 2x, k-tbl, p2; repeat from * an additional 3x.

Round 8: *K2tog, YO, p2, [k-tbl, p1] 3x, k2tog, [p1, k-tbl] 2x, YO, p2, YO, SSK, p2, YO, [k-tbl, p1] 2x, SSK, [p1, k-tbl] 3x, p2; repeat from *.

Round 9: *K2, p2, [k-tbl, p1] 5x, k-tbl, k1, p2, k2, p2, k1, [k-tbl, p1] 5x, k-tbl, p2; repeat from *.

Round 10: *YO, SSK, p2, [k-tbl, p1] 2x, k-tbl, k2tog, [p1, k-tbl] 2x, YO, k-tbl, p2, k2tog, YO, p2, k-tbl, YO, [k-tbl, p1] 2x, SSK, [k-tbl, p1] 2x, k-tbl, p2; repeat from *.

Round 11: *K2, p2, [k-tbl, p1] 2x, k-tbl 2x, [p1, k-tbl] 3x, p2, k2, p2, [k-tbl, p1] 3x, k-tbl 2x, [p1, k-tbl] 2x, p2; repeat from *.

Round 12: *K2tog, YO, p2, [k-tbl, p1] 2x, k2tog, [p1, k-tbl] 2x, YO, p1, k-tbl, p2, YO, SSK, p2, k-tbl, p1, YO, [k-tbl, p1] 2x, SSK, [p1, k-tbl] 2x, p2; repeat from *.

Round 13: *K2, p2, [k-tbl, p1] 4x, k-tbl, k1, p1, k-tbl, p2, k2, p2, k-tbl, p1, k1, [k-tbl, p1] 4x, k-tbl, p2; repeat from *.

Round 14: *YO, SSK, p2, k-tbl, p1, k-tbl, k2tog, [p1, k-tbl] 2x, YO, k-tbl, p1, k-tbl, p2, k2tog, YO, p2, k-tbl, p1, k-tbl, YO, [k-tbl, p1] 2x, SSK, k-tbl, p1, k-tbl, p2; repeat from *.

Round 15: *K2, p2, k-tbl, p1, k-tbl 2x, [p1, k-tbl] 4x, p2, k2, p2, [k-tbl, p1] 4x, k-tbl 2x, p1, k-tbl, p2; repeat from *.

Round 16: *K2tog, YO, p2, k-tbl, p1, k2tog, [p1, k-tbl] 2x, YO, [p1, k-tbl] 2x, p2, YO, SSK, p2, [k-tbl, p1] 2x, YO, [k-tbl, p1] 2x, SSK, p1, k-tbl, p2; repeat from *.

Round 17: *K2, p2, [k-tbl, p1] 3x, k-tbl, k1, [p1, k-tbl] 2x, p2, k2, p2, [k-tbl, p1] 2x, k1, [k-tbl, p1] 3x, k-tbl, p2; repeat from *.

Round 18: *YO, SSK, p2, k-tbl, k2tog, [p1, k-tbl] 2x, YO, [k-tbl, p1] 2x, k-tbl, p2, k2tog, YO, p2, [k-tbl, p1] 2x, k-tbl, YO, [k-tbl, p1] twice, SSK, k-tbl, p2; repeat from *.

Round 19: *K2, p2, k-tbl 2x, [p1, k-tbl] 5x, p2, k2, p2, [k-tbl, p1] 5x, k-tbl 2x, p2; repeat from *.

Round 20: *K2tog, YO, p2, k2tog, [p1, k-tbl] 2x, YO, [p1, k-tbl] 3x, p2, YO, SSK, p2, [k-tbl, p1] 3x, YO, [k-tbl, p1] 2x, SSK, p2; repeat from *.

Round 21: *K2, p2, [k-tbl, p1] 2x, k-tbl, p2, [k-tbl, p1] 2x, k-tbl, p2; repeat from * an additional 3x.

Round 22: *YO, SSK, [p2, T2F, k-tbl, T2B] 2x, p2, k2tog, YO, [p2, T2F, k-tbl, T2B] 2x, p2; repeat from *.

Round 23: Repeat Round 5.

Round 24: Repeat Round 4.

Rounds 25-31: Repeat Rounds 1-7.

Round 32: *K2tog, YO, p2, YO, [k-tbl, p1] 2x, SSK, [p1, k-tbl] 3x, p2, YO, SSK, p2, [k-tbl, p1] 3x, k2tog, [p1, k-tbl] 2x, YO, p2; repeat from *.

Round 33: *K2, p2, k1, [k-tbl, p1] 5x, k-tbl, p2, k2, p2, [k-tbl, p1] 5x, k-tbl, k1, p2; repeat from *.

Round 34: *YO, SSK, p2, k-tbl, YO, [k-tbl, p1] 2x, SSK, [k-tbl, p1] 2x, k-tbl, p2, k2tog, YO, p2, [k-tbl, p1] 2x, k-tbl, k2tog, [p1, k-tbl] twice, YO, k-tbl, p2; repeat from *.

Round 35: *K2, p2, [k-tbl, p1] 3x, k-tbl 2x, [p1, k-tbl] 2x, p2, k2, p2, [k-tbl, p1] 2x, k-tbl 2x, [p1, k-tbl] 3x, p2; repeat from *.

Round 36: *K2tog, YO, p2, k-tbl, p1, YO, [k-tbl, p1] 2x, SSK, [p1, k-tbl] 2x, p2, YO, SSK, p2, [k-tbl, p1] 2x, k2tog, [p1, k-tbl] 2x, YO, p1, k-tbl, p2; repeat from *.

Round 37: *K2, p2, k-tbl, p1, k1, [k-tbl, p1] 4x, k-tbl, p2, k2, p2, [k-tbl, p1] 4x, k-tbl, k1, p1, k-tbl, p2; repeat from *.

Round 38: *YO, SSK, p2, k-tbl, p1, k-tbl, YO, [k-tbl, p1] 2x, SSK, k-tbl, p1, k-tbl, p2, k2tog, YO, p2, k-tbl, p1, k-tbl, k2tog, [p1, k-tbl] 2x, YO, k-tbl, p1, k-tbl, p2; repeat from *.

Round 39: *K2, p2, [k-tbl, p1] 4x, k-tbl 2x, p1, k-tbl, p2, k2, p2, k-tbl, p1, k-tbl 2x, [p1, k-tbl] 4x, p2; repeat from *.

Round 40: *K2tog, YO, p2, [k-tbl, p1] 2x, YO, [k-tbl, p1] 2x, SSK, p1, k-tbl, p2, YO, SSK, p2, k-tbl, p1, k2tog, [p1, k-tbl] 2x, YO, [p1, k-tbl] 2x, p2; repeat from *.

Round 41: *K2, p2, [k-tbl, p1] 2x, k1, [k-tbl, p1] 3x, k-tbl, p2, k2, p2, [k-tbl, p1] 3x, k-tbl, k1, [p1, k-tbl] 2x, p2; repeat from *.

Round 42: *YO, SSK, p2, [k-tbl, p1] 2x, k-tbl, YO, [k-tbl, p1] 2x, SSK, k-tbl, p2, k2tog, YO, p2, k-tbl, k2tog, [p1, k-tbl] 2x, YO, [k-tbl, p1] 2x, k-tbl, p2; repeat from *.

Round 43: *K2, p2, [k-tbl, p1] 5x, k-tbl 2x, p2, k2, p2, k-tbl 2x, [p1, k-tbl] 5x, p2; repeat from *.

Round 44: *K2tog, YO, p2, [k-tbl, p1] 3x, YO, [k-tbl, p1] 2x, SSK, p2, YO, SSK, p2, k2tog, [p1, k-tbl] 2x, YO, [p1, k-tbl] 3x, p2; repeat from *.

Rounds 45-48: Repeat Rounds 21-24.

Heel Flap

Work across instep stitches in pattern. The heel flap will now be worked back-and-forth over the 34 heel stitches as follows (or from chart on p. 59):

Row 1 (RS): Sl1, p2, sl-left, p4, sl-left, p3, YO, SSK, p3, sl-left, p4, sl-left, p3.

Row 2 (WS): Sl1, k2, p3, k4, p3, k3, p2, k3, p3, k4, p3, k3.

Row 3: Sl1, p2, k3, p4, k3, p3, k2tog, YO, p3, k3, p4, k3, p3.

Row 4: Repeat Row 2.

Row 5: Repeat Row 1.

Row 6: Sl1, k2, p-tbl 3x, k4, p-tbl 3x, k3, p2, k3, p-tbl 3x, k4, p-tbl 3x, k3.

Row 7: Sl1, p1, [T2B, k-tbl, T2F, p2] 2x, k2tog, YO, [p2, T2B, k-tbl, T2F] 2x, p2.

Row 8: Sl1, k1, *[p-tbl, k1] 2x, p-tbl, k2; repeat from *, p2, **k2, [p-tbl, k1] 2x, p-tbl; repeat from **, k2.

Row 9: Sl1, p1, YO, [k-tbl, p1] 2x, SSK, [p1, k-tbl] 3x, p2, YO, SSK, p2, [k-tbl, p1] 3x, k2tog, [p1, k-tbl] 2x, YO, p2.

Row 10: Sl1, k1, p1, [p-tbl, k1] 5x, p-tbl, k2, p2, k2, [p-tbl, k1] 5x, p-tbl, p1, k2.

Row 11: Sl1, p1, k-tbl, YO, [k-tbl, p1] 2x, SSK, [k-tbl, p1] 2x, k-tbl, p2, k2tog, YO, p2, [k-tbl, p1] 2x, k-tbl, k2tog, [p1, k-tbl] 2x, YO, k-tbl, p2.

Row 12: Sl1, k1, [p-tbl, k1] 3x, p-tbl 2x, [k1, p-tbl] 2x, k2, p2, k2, [p-tbl, k1] 2x, p-tbl 2x, [k1, p-tbl] 3x, k2.

Row 13: Sl1, p1, k-tbl, p1, YO, [k-tbl, p1] 2x, SSK, [p1, k-tbl] 2x, p2, YO, SSK, p2, [k-tbl, p1] 2x, k2tog, [p1, k-tbl] 2x, YO, p1, k-tbl, p2.

Row 14: Sl1, k1, p-tbl, k1, p1, [p-tbl, k1] 4x, p-tbl, k2, p2, k2, [p-tbl, k1] 4x, p-tbl, p1, k1, p-tbl, k2.

Row 15: Sl1, p1, k-tbl, p1, k-tbl, YO, [k-tbl, p1] 2x, SSK, k-tbl, p1, k-tbl, p2, k2tog, YO, p2, k-tbl, p1, k-tbl, k2tog, [p1, k-tbl] 2x, YO, k-tbl, p1, k-tbl, p2.

Row 16: Sl1, k1, [p-tbl, k1] 4x, p-tbl 2x, k1, p-tbl, k2, p2, k2, p-tbl, k1, p-tbl 2x, [k1, p-tbl] 4x, k2.

Row 17: Sl1, p1, [k-tbl, p1] 2x, YO, [k-tbl, p1] 2x, SSK, p1, k-tbl, p2, YO, SSK, p2, k-tbl, p1, k2tog, [p1, k-tbl] 2x, YO, [p1, k-tbl] 2x, p2.

Row 18: Sl1, k1, [p-tbl, k1] 2x, p1, [p-tbl, k1] 3x, p-tbl, k2, p2, k2, [p-tbl, k1] 3x, p-tbl, p1, [k1, p-tbl] 2x, k2.

Row 19: Sl1, p1, [k-tbl, p1] 2x, k-tbl, YO, [k-tbl, p1] 2x, SSK, k-tbl, p2, k2tog, YO, p2, k-tbl, k2tog, [p1, k-tbl] 2x, YO, p2, k-tbl, k2tog, [p1, k-tbl] 2x, YO, [k-tbl, p1] 2x, k-tbl, p2.

Row 20: Sl1, k1, [p-tbl, k1] 5x, p-tbl 2x, k2, p2, k2, p-tbl 2x, [k1, p-tbl] 5x, k2.

Row 21: Sl1, p1, [k-tbl, p1] 3x, YO, [k-tbl, p1] 2x, SSK, p2, YO, SSK, p2, k2tog, [p1, k-tbl] 2x, YO, [p1, k-tbl] 3x, p2.
Row 22: Sl1, k1, *[p-tbl, k1] 2x, p-tbl, k2; repeat from *, p2, k2, **[p-tbl, k1] 2x, p-tbl, k2; repeat from **.
Row 23: Sl1, p1, [T2F, k-tbl, T2B, p2] 2x, k2tog, YO, [p2, T2F, k-tbl, T2B] 2x, p2.
Row 24: Repeat Row 6.
Rows 25-30: Repeat Rows 1-6.

Turn Heel
Row 1 (RS): Sl1, k18, SSK, k1, turn.
Row 2: Sl1, p5, p2tog, p1, turn.
Row 3: Sl1, knit to stitch before gap formed by previous row's turn, SSK, k1, turn.
Row 4: Sl1, purl to stitch before gap formed by previous row's turn, p2tog, p1, turn.
Repeat Rows 3-4 until all heel flap stitches have been worked. 20 heel stitches remain.

Shape Gusset
Knit across the 20 heel stitches. Working up the side of the heel flap with the same needle, pu 15 stitches. Work instep stitches in pattern as established. Working down the other side of the heel flap with an empty dpn or empty end of second circular needle, pu 15 stitches. 50 heel stitches.

If using dpns, knit the first 10 stitches from the second heel needle onto the

first so there are an equal number of heel stitches on each needle.

To get back to the beginning of the round, knit to the end of the heel stitches.

Round 1: Work instep stitches in pattern as established; knit to last 3 heel stitches, k2tog, k1.
Round 2: Work instep stitches in pattern as established; k1, SSK, knit to end of heel stitches. 48 heel stitches.
Repeat Rounds 1-2 an additional 7x. 34 heel stitches, 72 total stitches.

Foot
Continue to work instep stitches in pattern as established and heel stitches in stockinette stitch until foot from start of heel turn to needles measures approximately 2" less than desired finished bottom-of-foot length, ending on Round 1 or Round 25 if possible.

Toe
Round 1: Knit.
Round 2: *K1, SSK, knit to last 3 instep stitches, k2tog, k1; knit across heel stitches. 70 stitches.
Repeat Rounds 1-2 once more. 68 stitches, 34 instep and 34 heel.

Round 3: Knit.

Round 4: *K1, SSK, knit to last 3 instep stitches, k2tog, k1; repeat from * across heel stitches. 64 stitches.
Repeat Rounds 3-4 an additional 7x. 36 stitches. Then, repeat Round 4 only an additional 4x. 20 stitches.

Cut yarn, leaving a 14-16" tail. Graft toe closed using Kitchener Stitch.

Finishing
Weave in any remaining ends, dampen socks and lay flat to block or use sock blockers.

Curtain Pattern - Rounds 1-24

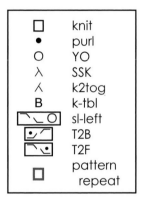

Legend:
- ☐ knit
- • purl
- O YO
- λ SSK
- ⋏ k2tog
- B k-tbl
- sl-left
- T2B
- T2F
- ☐ pattern repeat

Curtain Pattern - Rounds 25-48

Legend:
- □ knit
- ● purl
- ○ YO
- λ SSK
- ⅄ k2tog
- B k-tbl
- ⌐⌐○ sl-left
- T2B
- T2F
- □ pattern repeat

Heel Flap Chart

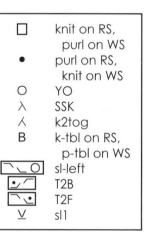

Materials:

Approximately 400 yards of fingering-weight yarn, 25-100 yards of several colors. *Sample uses Elemental Affects Natural Shetland Fingering in 'Forest Moss', 'Musket', 'Lime Juice', 'Lichen', 'Yellow' and 'Fawn'.*

US1 (2.25mm) needles or size needed to obtain gauge

Yarn needle

Gauge:

8 stitches/11 rounds per inch in colorwork pattern

Size:

Foot circumference = approximately 8"

Natsa Sukka

Designer's Notes:

I became obsessed with this rustic Shetland wool yarn after Jeane, the brains behind Elemental Affects, showed me the amazing results she got by using the same light yellow dye on different shades of natural wool. You can see several of the resulting skeins (flanked by a couple of undyed siblings) in the photo on the opposite page. The lemon yellow skein was dyed on a cream base, while the deeper greens were a result of using the same dye on the darker bases. I was amazed that those diverse shades all came from the same lemon yellow dye!

I had to make textured color-work socks from this yarn. They are designed to be worked top-down or toe-up, with a color arrangement that's totally up to you. I opted for ankle-length slipper socks to make knitting them less of a commitment, but if you're up to it, they would also look spectacular with full-length cuffs.

Natsa Sukka translates roughly as "stripe sock" in Finnish, the tongue of my grandfathers. I couldn't find the Finnish word for chevrons!

Toe-Up Version

Using Judy's Magic Cast-On or your favorite toe-up cast on and the color you'd like to use for the toe, cast on 8 instep stitches and 8 heel stitches (16 total stitches), dividing them over your selected needles.

Round 1: Knit.
Round 2: *K-fb, knit to last 2 instep stitches, k-fb, k1; repeat from * across heel stitches. 20 stitches.
Repeat Round 2 only an additional 2x. 28 stitches. Then, repeat Rounds 1-2 an additional 9x. 64 stitches, 32 instep and 32 heel.

Foot

Begin working all stitches in *Color Pattern* from chart, using the six colors in any order you'd like. You can keep the colors in the same order for every repeat, or change them around as shown in the sample. Work until foot measures 2" less than desired finished length from tip of toe.

Heel

Work across instep stitches in pattern. Join color to be used for heel. You can leave the colors being used for the foot attached so that you can pick them up and continue with the color pattern once the heel is complete.

Color Pattern

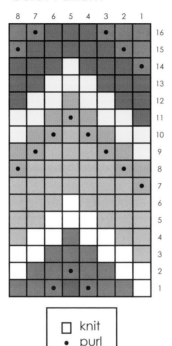

```
□  knit
•  purl
```

The heel turn will now be worked back-and-forth over the 32 heel stitches.

Shape Bottom of Heel

Row 1 (RS): K31, W&T.
Row 2 (WS): P30, W&T.
Row 3: Knit to stitch before wrapped stitch (do not knit any wrapped stitches), W&T.
Row 4: Purl to stitch before wrapped stitch (do not purl any wrapped stitches), W&T.

Repeat Rows 3-4 an additional 9x – there are now 11 wrapped stitches on either side of 10 unwrapped center stitches.

Shape Top of Heel

Row 1 (RS): Knit to first wrapped stitch (do not knit across any wrapped stitches), lift wrap RS, turn.
Row 2 (WS): Purl to first wrapped stitch (do not purl across any wrapped stitches), lift wrap WS, turn.
Row 3: Sl1, knit to next wrapped stitch (just past the stitch unwrapped on the previous RS row), lift wrap RS, turn.
Row 4: Sl1, purl to next wrapped stitch (just past the stitch unwrapped on the previous WS row), lift wrap WS, turn.

Repeat Rows 3-4 an additional 8x – a single wrapped stitch remains on either side of heel. Drop heel color and pick up colors being used for pattern.

Next Row: Sl1, work in *Color Pattern* as established to last wrapped stitch, lift wrap RS but do not turn. You should be at the beginning of the instep stitches.
Next Round: Work instep stitches in *Color Pattern*; lift wrap RS, continue in *Color Pattern* to end of heel stitches.

Leg

Work even in pattern until leg measures approximately 1" from top of heel or 1" less than desired finished leg length.

Cuff

Break colors being used for leg and join color to be used for cuff. Knit one round even. Then, work in k2, p2 rib for 1". Break cuff color and join contrast color for bind-off.

Bind off all stitches loosely as follows: K1, *YO, k1, using tip of left needle, pass 2nd and 3rd stitches on right needle over 1st stitch on right needle (one stitch remains on right needle); repeat from * until all stitches are bound off. Fasten off.

Finishing

Weave in any remaining ends, dampen socks and lay flat to block or use sock blockers.

Top-Down Version

With contrast color, cast on 64 stitches and divide them over dpns or circular needles as follows:
- If using dpns, place 16 stitches on each of four needles.
- If using circular needle(s), place 32 stitches on each needle.

The first 32 stitches of the round are the instep stitches and the last 32 stitches are the heel stitches. Join stitches into round being careful not to twist.

Cuff

Break contrast color and join color to be used for cuff. Work in k2, p2 rib for 1".

Leg

Begin working all stitches in *Color Pattern* from chart, using the six colors in any order you'd like. You can keep the colors in the same order for every repeat, or change them around as shown in the sample. Work until leg measures 2" from cast-on edge or desired length to top of heel.

Heel

Work as for toe-up sock (in this case, the Shape Bottom of Heel section will actually be the top of the heel and vice versa).

Foot

Work even in pattern until foot measures 2" less than desired finished length. Break colors being used for foot and join color to be used for toe.

Toe

Round 1: Knit.
Round 2: *K1, SSK, knit to last 3 instep stitches, k2tog, k1; repeat from * across heel stitches. 60 stitches.

Repeat Rounds 1-2 an additional 8x. 28 stitches. Then, repeat Round 2 only an additional 3x. 16 stitches.

Cut yarn, leaving a 14-16" tail. Graft toe closed using Kitchener stitch.

Finishing

Finish as for toe-up sock.

Picot

La Libera

95%Merino / 5% Nylon   100g / 3.53oz

8 sts/in. on US0-3   360 yards

Materials:

Approximately 380 yards of fingering-weight yarn. *Sample uses Pico(t) La Libera (80% superwash merino wool, 20% nylon) in 'Gwendolyn'.*

US1 (2.25mm) needles or size needed to obtain gauge

Yarn needle

Gauge:

9 stitches/12 rounds per inch in stockinette stitch

Size:

Foot circumference = approximately 7-1/2 (9)"

Vinings

Designer's Notes:

This fetching naturally-dyed yarn created by Portland resident Stevanie Pico reminds me of mossy forest floors and dappled sunlight filtering through treetops, a common sight in Stevanie's (and my!) Pacific Northwest.

I had to put leaves on these socks, and seeded rib panels provide the perfect interlude between the falling leaves down the front and climbing vines up the back. They are named after the neighborhood in Atlanta, Georgia, where my husband and I lived shortly after we were married - another place where tall trees and thick vegetation reign supreme.

The diagonal movement at the edges of the leaves and the purl stitches interspersed down the seeded ribs help to break up the small color variations in the yarn. I would recommend a light-colored semi-solid or very slightly variegated colorway for these socks. The leaf pattern running down the front panel tends to disappear in a stronger-colored yarn.

This was the May 2011 Indie Socks CSK featured pattern.

Toe

Using Judy's Magic Cast-On or your favorite toe-up cast on, cast on 9 (11) instep stitches and 9 (11) heel stitches (18, (22) total stitches), dividing them over your selected needles.

Round 1: Knit.
Round 2: *K-fb, knit to last 2 instep stitches, k-fb, k1; repeat from * across heel stitches. 22 (26) stitches. Repeat Round 2 only an additional 3x. 34 (38) stitches. Then, repeat Rounds 1-2 an additional 8 (11)x. 66 (82) stitches, 33 (41) instep and 33 (41) heel. Knit one round even.

Foot

Begin working *Instep Pattern* Rounds 1-8 as follows (or from chart on p. 68) across the instep stitches. Continue working heel stitches in stockinette stitch.

Instep Pattern

(over 33 (41) stitches and 8 rounds)
Round 1: [P1, k1] 4 (6)x, [YO, k1] 2x, SSK, p1, k2tog, k1, p1, k1, SSK, p1, k2tog, [k1, YO] 2x, [k1, p1] 4 (6)x.
Round 2: [P1, k3] 1 (2)x, p1, k8, [p1, k2] 2x, p1, k8, p1, [k3, p1] 1 (2)x.
Round 3: [P1, k1] 4 (6)x, YO, k3, YO, SSK, p1, k2tog, p1, SSK, p1, k2tog, YO, k3, YO, [k1, p1] 4, (6)x.

Round 4: [P1, k3] 1 (2)x, p1, k9, [p1, k1] 2x, p1, k9, p1, [k3, p1] 1 (2)x.
Round 5: [P1, k1] 4 (6)x, YO, k5, YO, SK2P, p1, k3tog, YO, k5, YO, [k1, p1] 4 (6)x.
Round 6: [P1, k3] 1 (2)x, p1, k11, p1, k11, p1, [k3, p1] 1 (2)x.
Round 7: [P1, k1] 4 (6)x, YO, k3, p1, k2tog, k1, YO, SK2P, YO, k1, SSK, p1, k3, YO, [k1, p1] 4 (6)x.
Round 8: [P1, k3] 1 (2)x, [p1, k7] 3x, p1, [k3, p1] 1 (2)x.

Repeat Rounds 1-8 until foot measures approximately 3-1/2 (4-3/4)" less than desired finished foot length (you can end on any pattern round).

Gusset

Round 1: Work instep stitches in *Instep Pattern* as established; k-fb in first heel stitch, knit to last 2 heel stitches, k-fb, k1.
Round 2: Work instep stitches in *Instep Pattern* as established; knit across all heel stitches.
Repeat Rounds 1-2 an additional 10 (14)x, then work Round 1 once more. 57 (73) heel stitches.

Turn Heel

Work across instep stitches in pattern. The heel turn will be worked back-and-forth over the 57 (73) heel stitches.
Row 1 (RS): K44 (56), W&T.
Row 2 (WS): P31 (39), W&T.

Row 3: Knit to stitch before wrapped stitch (do not knit any wrapped stitches), W&T.
Row 4: Purl to stitch before wrapped stitch (do not purl any wrapped stitches), W&T.
Repeat Rows 3-4 an additional 9 (11)x – there are now 11 (13) wrapped stitches on either side of 11 (15) unwrapped center stitches.

Knit to end of heel stitches, lifting wraps RS as they are encountered, then work across instep stitches in pattern.

Heel Flap

Work the heel flap back and forth as follows (or from the charts on p. 69):
Row 1 (RS): K44 (56), lifting remaining wraps RS as you encounter them, SSK, turn.
Row 2 (WS): Sl1, p2, [k1, p3] 1 (2)x, k1, p17, [k1, p3] 1 (2)x, k1, p2, p2tog, turn. 33 (41) center heel stitches.
Row 3: Sl1, [p1, k1] 3 (5)x, p1, k5, k2tog, YO, k1, YO, k3, YO, k1, YO, k2, SSK, k1, [p1, k1] 3 (5)x, p1, SSK, turn. 35 (43) center heel stitches.
Row 4: Sl1, p2, [k1, p3] 1 (2)x, k1, SSP, p11, p2tog, p4, [k1, p3] 1 (2)x, k1, p2, p2tog, turn. 33 (41) center heel stitches.
Row 5: Sl1, [p1, k1] 3 (5)x, p1, k3, k2tog, [k1, YO] 2x, k10, [p1, k1] 3 (5)x, p1, SSK, turn. 34 (42) center heel stitches.

Row 6: Sl1, p2, [k1, p3] 1 (2)x, k1, p14, p2tog, p2, [k1, p3] 1 (2)x, k1, p2, p2tog, turn. 33 (41) center heel stitches.

Row 7: Sl1, [p1, k1] 3 (5)x, p1, k1, k2tog, k2, YO, k1, YO, k3, YO, k1, YO, SSK, k5, [p1, k1] 3 (5)x, p1, SSK, turn. 35 (43) center heel stitches.

Row 8: Sl1, p2, [k1, p3] 1 (2)x, k1, p4, SSP, p11, p2tog, [k1, p3] 1 (2)x, k1, p2, p2tog, turn. 33 (41) center heel stitches.

Row 9: Sl1, [p1, k1] 3 (5)x, p1, k10, [YO, k1] 2x, SSK, k3, [p1, k1] 3 (5)x, p1, SSK, turn. 34 (42) center heel stitches.

Row 10: Sl1, p2, [k1, p3] 1 (2)x, k1, p2, SSP, p14, [k1, p3] 1 (2)x, k1, p2, p2tog, turn. 33 (41) center heel stitches.

Rows 11-18: Repeat Rows 3-10.

Rows 19-22: Repeat Rows 3-6.

7-1/4" size only -

Row 23: Repeat Row 7. 35 total heel stitches. Do not turn after working Row 23.

Round 24: Work across instep stitches in pattern; k2tog, k2, p1, k3, p1,k2tog, k11, SSK, k4, [p1, k3] 2x. 66 stitches, 33 instep and 33 heel.

9" size only -

Rows 23-26: Repeat Rows 7-10.

Rows 27-31: Repeat Rows 3-7. 43 total heel stitches. Do not turn after working Row 31.

Round 32: Work across instep stitches in pattern; k2tog, k2, [p1, k3] 2x, p1, k2tog, k11, SSK, k4, [p1, k3] 3x. 82 stitches, 41 instep and 41 heel.

Leg

Continue to work the instep stitches in pattern as established. Begin working the heel stitches in *Back Leg Pattern* as follows (or from chart on p. 68), starting with Round 5 for 7-1/4" size or Round 1 for 9" size.

Back Leg Pattern

(over 33-35 (41-43) stitches and 8 rounds)

Round 1: [K1, p1] 4 (6)x, k10, [YO, k1] 2x, SSK, k3, [p1, k1] 4 (6)x. 34 (42) stitches.

Round 2: [K3, p1] 2 (3)x, k14, SSK, k2, [p1, k3] 2 (3)x. 33 (41) stitches.

Round 3: [K1, p1] 4 (6)x, k5, k2tog, YO, k1, YO, k3, YO, k1, YO, k2, SSK, k1, [p1, k1] 4 (6)x. 35 (43) stitches.

Round 4: [K3, p1] 2 (3)x, k4, k2tog, k11, SSK, [p1, k3] 2 (3)x. 33 (41) stitches.

Round 5: [K1, p1] 4 (6)x, k3, k2tog, [k1, YO] 2x, k10, [p1, k1] 4 (6)x. 34 (42) stitches.

Round 6: [K3, p1] 2 (3)x, k2, k2tog, k14, [p1, k3] 2 (3)x. 33 (41) stitches.

Round 7: [K1, p1] 4 (6)x, k1, k2tog, k2, YO, k1, YO, k3, YO, k1, YO, SSK, k5, [p1, k1] 4 (6)x. 35 (43) stitches.

Round 8: [K3, p1] 2 (3)x, k2tog, k11, SSK, k4, [p1, k3] 2 (3)x. 33 (41) stitches.

Work in pattern until the leg measures approximately 5" from top of heel flap (or 1/2" less than desired finished length).

Cuff

Round 1: Purl.
Round 2: Knit.
Round 3: Purl.
Round 4: Knit.
Round 5: Purl.

Bind off all stitches loosely as follows: K1, *YO, k1, using tip of left needle, pass 2nd and 3rd stitches on right needle over 1st stitch on right needle (one stitch remains on right needle); repeat from * until all stitches are bound off. Fasten off.

Finishing

Weave in any remaining ends, dampen socks and lay flat to block or use sock blockers.

Instep Pattern

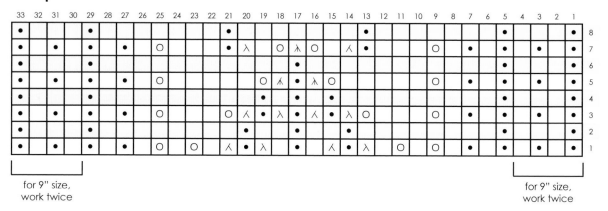

for 9" size,
work twice

for 9" size,
work twice

Back Leg Pattern

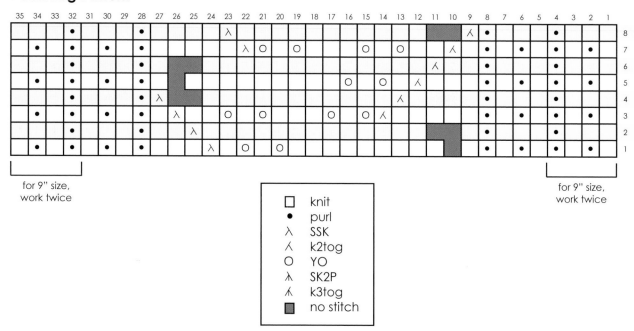

for 9" size,
work twice

for 9" size,
work twice

□	knit
•	purl
λ	SSK
⅄	k2tog
O	YO
λ	SK2P
⅄	k3tog
■	no stitch

Heel Flap Pattern (7-1/2" size)

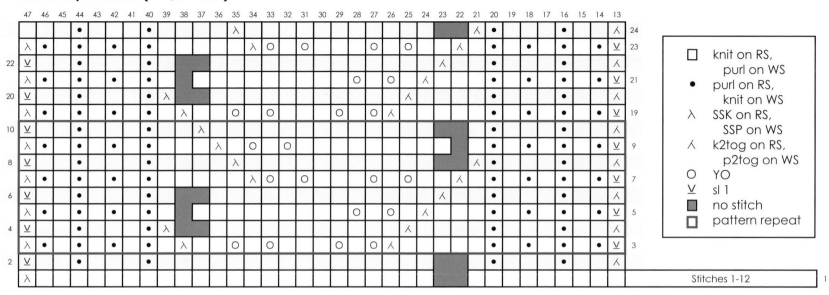

Heel Flap Pattern (9" size)

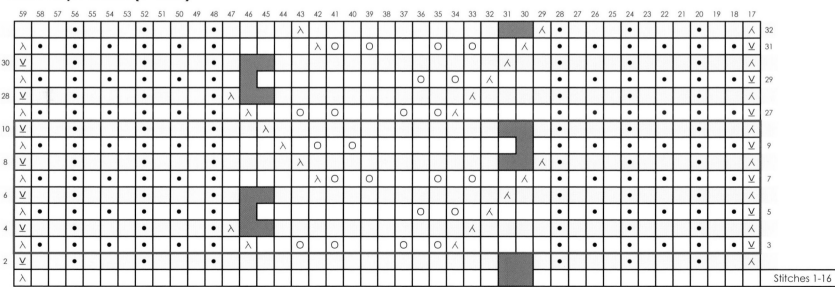

stitchjones

HAND-DYED YARN AND FIBER

COLOR GOES TO ELEVEN

Materials:

Approximately 400 yards of fingering-weight yarn. *Sample uses Stitchjones 100% Merino Sock (100% superwash merino wool) in 'Crush'.*

US1 (2.25mm) needles or size needed to obtain gauge

Yarn needle

Gauge:

9 stitches/12 rounds per inch in stockinette stitch

Size:

Foot circumference = approximately 8"

Orange Blossom

Designer's Notes:

All of my friends know that I have a soft spot for orange. In fact, when I first started my pattern line, I paged through my first catalog and realized that half the designs were orange (the other half were purple)!

The dyer behind Stitchjones, my friend Sharon, worked with me for several months at one of our local yarn shops and knows first-hand about my passion for orange. She hand-picked this colorway for me because she knew I wouldn't be able to resist it (and of course, she was right!).

I know that orange is a color people either love or hate, so if it's not your thing, this design will look just as spectacular in a number of different colors. I designed it around a plant theme, with cat's paw lace on the front (this motif is very reminiscent of the blossoms on the mock orange in our front yard) and a cascade of leaves running down the back of the leg and the heel flap. Green would be another obvious choice for these nature-inspired beauties.

Special Abbreviations and Techniques for This Pattern

C1/2F: Sl1 to cable needle and hold in front, k2, k1 from cable needle

C1/2B: Sl2 to cable needle and hold in back, k1, k2 from cable needle

Leg

Cast on 71 stitches and divide them over dpns or circular needles as follows:

- If using dpns, place 19 stitches on needle 1, 16 stitches on needle 2, 14 stitches on needle 3, and 22 stitches on needle 4.
- If using circular needle(s), place 35 stitches on needle 1 and 36 stitches on needle 2.

The first 35 stitches of the round are the instep stitches and the last 36 stitches are the heel stitches. Join stitches into round being careful not to twist.

Begin working *Orange Blossom Rib Pattern* across the 35 instep stitches, and *Back Leg Pattern* across the 36 heel stitches as follows (or from charts on p. 75-76) :

Orange Blossom Rib Pattern

(over 35 stitches and 20 rounds)
Round 1: P1, [k3, YO, S2KP, YO, k3, p3] 2x, k3, YO, S2KP, YO, k3, p1.
Round 2: P1, [k9, p3] 2x, k9, p1.
Round 3: P1, [k1, k2tog, YO, k3, YO, SSK, k1, p3] 2x, k1, k2tog, YO, k3, YO, SSK, k1, p1.
Round 4: P1, [k9, p3] 2x, k9, p1.
Rounds 5-8: Repeat Rounds 1-4.
Round 9: P1, [k3, YO, S2KP, YO, k3, p3] 2x, k3, YO, S2KP, YO, k3, p1.
Round 10: P1, [k3, p3] 5x, k3, p1.
Round 11: P1, k3, [p3, k3, YO, S2KP, YO, k3] 2x, p3, k3, p1.
Round 12: P1, k3, [p3, k9] 2x, p3, k3, p1.
Round 13: P1, k3, [p3, k1, k2tog, YO, k3, YO, SSK, k1] 2x, p3, k3, p1.
Round 14: P1, k3, [p3, k9] 2x, p3, k3, p1.
Round 15-18: Repeat Rounds 11-14.
Round 19: P1, k3, [p3, k3, YO, S2KP, YO, k3] 2x, p3, k3, p1.
Round 20: P1, [k3, p3] 5x, k3, p1.

Back Leg Pattern

(over 32-36 stitches and 20 rounds)
Round 1: P1, k7, p3, T2B, p1, k2, p3, SSK, k3, k2tog, p2, k7, p1. 34 stitches.
Round 2: P1, k7, p3, k1, p2, k2, p3, k5, p2, k7, p1.
Round 3: P1, C1/2B, k1, C1/2F, p2, T2B, p2, k2, p3, SSK, k1, k2tog, p2, C1/2B, k1, C1/2F, p1. 32 stitches.
Round 4: P1, k7, p2, k1, p3, k2, p3, k3, p2, k7, p1.
Round 5: P1, k7, p2, YO, k1, YO, p3, k2, p3, S2KP, p2, k7, p1.
Round 6: P1, k7, p2, k3, p3, k2, p6, k7, p1.
Round 7: P1, C1/2B, k1, C1/2F, p2, [k1, YO] twice, k1, p3, k1, m1, k1, p2tog, p4, C1/2B, k1, C1/2F, p1. 34 stitches.
Round 8: P1, k7, p2, k5, p3, k3, p5, k7, p1.
Round 9: P1, k7, p2, k2, YO, k1, YO, k2, p3, k2, T2F, p4, k7, p1. 36 stitches.
Round 10: P1, k7, p2, k7, p3, k2, p1, k1, p4, k7, p1.
Round 11: P1, C1/2B, k1, C1/2F, p2, SSK, k3, k2tog, p3, k2, p1, T2F, p3, C1/2B, k1, C1/2F, p1. 34 stitches.
Round 12: P1, k7, p2, k5, p3, k2, p2, k1, p3, k7, p1.
Round 13: P1, k7, p2, SSK, k1, k2tog, p3, k2, p2, T2F, p2, k7, p1. 32 stitches.
Round 14: P1, k7, p2, k3, p3, k2, p3, k1, p2, k7, p1.
Round 15: P1, C1/2B, k1, C1/2F, p2, S2KP, p3, k2, p3, YO, k1, YO, p2, C1/2B, k1, C1/2F, p1.
Round 16: P1, k7, p6, k2, p3, k3, p2, k7, p1.
Round 17: P1, k7, p4, p2tog, k1, m1, k1, p3, [k1, YO] twice, k1, p2, k7, p1. 34 stitches.
Round 18: P1, k7, p5, k3, p3, k5, p2, k7, p1.
Round 19: P1, C1/2B, k1, C1/2F, p4, T2B, k2, p3, k2, YO, k1, YO, k2, p2, C1/2B, k1, C1/2F, p1. 36 stitches.
Round 20: P1, k7, p4, k1, p1, k2, p3, k7, p2, k7, p1.

Work in pattern until leg measures approximately 6" from start (or desired length to top of heel flap), ending with Round 20.

Heel Flap

Work across instep stitches in pattern. The heel flap will now be worked back-and-forth over the 36 heel stitches as follows (or from chart on p. 77):

Row 1 (RS): Sl1, k7, p3, T2B, p1, k2, p3, SSK, k3, k2tog, p2, k7, p1. 34 stitches.

Row 2 (WS): Sl1, p7, k2, p5, k3, p2, k2, p1, k3, p7, k1.

Row 3: Sl1, C1/2B, k1, C1/2F, p2, T2B, p2, k2, p3, SSK, k1, k2tog, p2, C1/2B, k1, C1/2F, p1. 32 stitches.

Row 4: Sl1, p7, k2, p3, k3, p2, k3, p1, k2, p7, k1.

Row 5: Sl1, k7, p2, YO, k1, YO, p3, k2, p3, S2KP, p2, k7, p1.

Row 6: Sl1, p7, k6, p2, k3, p3, k2, p7, k1.

Row 7: Sl1, C1/2B, k1, C1/2F, p2, [k1, YO] 2x, k1, p3, k1, m1, k1, p2tog, p4, C1/2B, k1, C1/2F, p1. 34 stitches.

Row 8: Sl1, p7, k5, p3, k3, p5, k2, p7, k1.

Row 9: Sl1, k7, p2, k2, YO, k1, YO, k2, p3, k2, T2F, p4, k7, p1. 36 stitches.

Row 10: Sl1, p7, k4, p1, k1, p2, k3, p7, k2, p7, k1.

Row 11: Sl1, C1/2B, k1, C1/2F, p2, SSK, k3, k2tog, p3, k2, p1, T2F, p3, C1/2B, k1, C1/2F, p1. 34 stitches.

Row 12: Sl1, p7, k3, p1, k2, p2, k3, p5, k2, p7, k1.

Row 13: Sl1, k7, p2, SSK, k1, k2tog, p3, k2, p2, T2F, p2, k7, p1. 32 stitches.

Row 14: Sl1, p7, k2, p1, k3, p2, k3, p3, k2, p7, k1.

Row 15: Sl1, C1/2B, k1, C1/2F, p2, S2KP, p3, k2, p3, YO, k1, YO, p2, C1/2B, k1, C1/2F, p1.

Row 16: Sl1, p7, k2, p3, k3, p2, k6, p7, k1.

Row 17: Sl1, k7, p4, p2tog, k1, m1, k1, p3, [k1, YO] 2x, k1, p2, k7, p1. 34 stitches.

Row 18: Sl1, p7, k2, p5, k3, p3, k5, p7, k1.

Row 19: Sl1, C1/2B, k1, C1/2F, p4, T2B, k2, p3, k2, YO, k1, YO, k2, p2, C1/2B, k1, C1/2F, p1. 36 stitches.

Row 20: Sl1, p7, k2, p7, k3, p2, k1, p1, k4, p7, k1.

Work Rows 1-20, then repeat Rows 1-8 once more for a total of 28 heel flap rows.

Turn Heel

Row 1 (RS): Sl1, k18, SSK, k1, turn.

Row 2: Sl1, p5, p2tog, p1, turn.

Row 3: Sl1, knit to stitch before gap formed by previous row's turn, SSK, k1, turn.

Row 4: Sl1, purl to stitch before gap formed by previous row's turn, p2tog, p1, turn.

Repeat Rows 3-4 until all heel flap stitches have been worked. 20 heel stitches remain.

Shape Gusset

Knit across the 20 heel stitches. Working up the side of the heel flap with the same needle, pu 14 stitches. Work instep stitches in pattern as established. Working down the other side of the heel flap with an empty dpn or empty end of second circular needle, pu 14 stitches. 48 heel stitches.

If using dpns, knit the first 10 stitches from the second heel needle onto the first so there are an equal number of heel stitches on each needle.

To get back to the beginning of the round, knit to the end of the heel stitches.

Round 1: Work instep stitches in pattern as established; knit to last 3 heel stitches, k2tog, k1.

Round 2: Work instep stitches in pattern as established; k1, SSK, knit to end of heel stitches. 46 heel stitches.

Repeat Rounds 1-2 an additional 5x, then work Round 1 once more. 35 heel stitches, 70 total stitches.

Foot

Continue to work instep stitches in pattern as established and heel stitches in stockinette stitch until foot from start of heel turn to needles measures approximately 2" less than desired finished bottom-of-foot length.

Toe

Round 1: Knit.

Round 2: *K16, k2tog, k15, k2tog; repeat from * across heel stitches. 66 stitches.

Round 3: Knit.

Round 4: *K15, k2tog, k14, k2tog; repeat from * across heel stitches. 62 stitches.

Round 5: Knit.

Round 6: *K14, k2tog, k13, k2tog; repeat from * across heel stitches. 58 stitches.

Round 7: Knit.

Round 8: *K13, k2tog, k12, k2tog; repeat from * across heel stitches. 54 stitches.

Round 9: Knit.

Round 10: *K12, k2tog, k11, k2tog; repeat from * across heel stitches. 50 stitches.

Round 11: Knit.

Round 12: *K11, k2tog, k10, k2tog; repeat from * across heel stitches. 46 stitches.

Round 13: Knit.

Round 14: *K10, k2tog, k9, k2tog; repeat from * across heel stitches. 42 stitches.

Round 15: Knit.

Round 16: *K9, k2tog, k8, k2tog; repeat from * across heel stitches. 38 stitches.

Round 17: *K8, k2tog, k7, k2tog; repeat from * across heel stitches. 34 stitches.

Round 18: Knit.

Round 19: *K7, k2tog, k6, k2tog; repeat from * across heel stitches. 30 stitches.

Round 20: *K6, k2tog, k5, k2tog; repeat from * across heel stitches. 26 stitches.

Round 21: *K5, k2tog, k4, k2tog; repeat from * across heel stitches. 22 stitches.

Round 22: *K4, k2tog, k3, k2tog; repeat from * across heel stitches. 18 stitches.

Round 23: *K3, k2tog, k2, k2tog; repeat from * across heel stitches.14 stitches.

Round 24: *K2, k2tog, k1, k2tog; repeat from * across heel stitches. 10 stitches.

Round 25: *K1, [k2tog] twice; repeat from * across heel stitches. 6 stitches.

Cut yarn, leaving an 8-10" tail. Thread tail through remaining stitches and pull tight. Weave in securely on WS of work.

Finishing

Weave in any remaining ends, dampen socks and lay flat to block or use sock blockers.

Orange Blossom Rib Pattern

35	34	33	32	31	30	29	28	27	26	25	24	23	22	21	20	19	18	17	16	15	14	13	12	11	10	9	8	7	6	5	4	3	2	1	Row
•				•	•	•				•	•	•				•	•	•				•	•	•				•	•	•				•	20
•				•	•	•				O	⋀	O				•	•	•				O	⋀	O				•	•	•				•	19
•				•	•	•										•	•	•										•	•	•				•	18
•				•	•	•		λ	O			O	人			•	•	•		λ	O				O	人		•	•	•				•	17
•				•	•	•										•	•	•										•	•	•				•	16
•				•	•	•				O	⋀	O				•	•	•				O	⋀	O				•	•	•				•	15
•				•	•	•										•	•	•										•	•	•				•	14
•				•	•	•		λ	O			O	人			•	•	•		λ	O				O	人		•	•	•				•	13
•				•	•	•										•	•	•										•	•	•				•	12
•				•	•	•				O	⋀	O				•	•	•				O	⋀	O				•	•	•				•	11
•										•	•	•										•	•	•										•	10
•				O	⋀	O				•	•	•				O	⋀	O				•	•	•				O	⋀	O				•	9
•										•	•	•										•	•	•										•	8
•		λ	O				O	人		•	•	•		λ	O				O	人		•	•	•		λ	O				O	人		•	7
•										•	•	•										•	•	•										•	6
•				O	⋀	O				•	•	•				O	⋀	O				•	•	•				O	⋀	O				•	5
•										•	•	•										•	•	•										•	4
•		λ	O				O	人		•	•	•		λ	O				O	人		•	•	•		λ	O				O	人		•	3
•										•	•	•										•	•	•										•	2
•				O	⋀	O				•	•	•				O	⋀	O				•	•	•				O	⋀	O				•	1

Symbol	Meaning
□	knit
•	purl
人	k2tog
λ	SSK
O	YO
⋀	S2KP

Back Leg Pattern

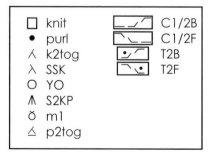

☐	knit	
●	purl	
人	k2tog	
入	SSK	
O	YO	
𝗔	S2KP	
ŏ	m1	
△	p2tog	

C1/2B	
C1/2F	
T2B	
T2F	

Heel Flap Pattern

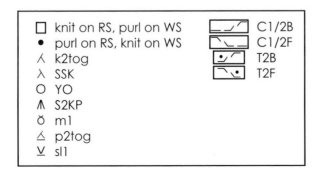

Symbol	Meaning
□	knit on RS, purl on WS
●	purl on RS, knit on WS
⋏	k2tog
⋌	SSK
O	YO
⋀	S2KP
ð	m1
△	p2tog
V	sl1
C1/2B	
C1/2F	
T2B	
T2F	

hazel knits

artisan sock

hand painted fingering yarn

90% superwash merino, *silk*

Materials:

Approximately 400 yards of fingering-weight yarn. *Sample uses Hazel Knits Artisan Sock (90% superwash merino wool, 10% nylon) in 'Wheatberry'*.

US1 (2.25mm) needles or size needed to obtain gauge

Yarn needle, 2 stitch markers

Gauge:

9 stitches/12 rounds per inch in stockinette stitch

Size:

Foot circumference = approximately 7-1/2"

Tulip Socks

Designer's Notes:

At the request of a friend, I created this sock using the Fountain Lace pattern from Barbara Walker's *A Second Treasury of Knitting Patterns*. This friend had recently finished knitting my Kiwassa Shawl pattern, which uses the same stitch, and wanted matching socks.

After a few false starts with yarns not suitable for the design, I decided to give this Hazel Knits semi-solid a try. Worked from the top down, the little lace umbrellas turn into small cups that remind me of tulips.

Since this lace pattern naturally forms points along the edge, I opted to emphasize them with a fun little picot edging at the top. Since the socks were already leaning toward the decorative side of the 'decorative vs functional' spectrum, I threw in my favorite star toe for good measure. It isn't the most anatomically correct toe you'll knit, but I think it's the most fun!

This was the August 2010 Indie Socks CSK featured pattern.

Special Abbreviations and Techniques for This Pattern

bobble: K-fbf, [turn, k3] 3x, turn, slip 2 stitches together as if to knit, k1, pass 2 slipped stitches over first stitch on right needle

Leg

Cast on 96 stitches and divide them over dpns or circular needles as follows:

- If using dpns, place 24 stitches on each needle.
- If using circular needle(s), place 48 stitches on each needle.

The first 48 stitches of the round are the instep stitches and the last 48 stitches are the heel stitches. Join stitches into round being careful not to twist.

Round 1: P4, [bobble, p8] 7x, bobble, p4. 64 stitches.
Round 2: Knit.
Round 3: Purl.

Begin working *Lace Pattern for Leg* as follows (or from chart on p. 82) across all stitches:

Lace Pattern for Leg

(over a multiple of 16 stitches and 8 rounds)
Round 1: Knit.
Round 2: *YO, k3, S2KP, k3, YO, k2tog, YO, k3, YO, SSK; repeat from * to end of round.
Round 3: Knit.
Round 4: *K1, YO, k2, S2KP, [k2, YO] 2x, k2tog, k1, SSK, YO, k1; repeat from * to end of round.
Round 5: Knit.
Round 6: *K2, YO, k1, S2KP, k1, YO, k3, YO, k2tog, k1, SSK, YO, k1; repeat from * to end of round.
Round 7: Knit.
Round 8: *K3, YO, S2KP, YO, k3, YO, SSK, YO, S2KP, YO, k2tog, YO; repeat from * to end of round.

Repeat Rounds 1-8 until leg measures approximately 5-1/2" from start (or desired length to top of heel flap), ending with Round 8 of pattern.

Heel Flap

K37, then place the next 31 stitches on a single needle (the heel needle). The remaining 33 stitches will be placed on a second circular or divided over two dpns for instep (12 on first dpn, 21 on second dpn). **The beginning of round position is shifted slightly.**

The heel flap will be worked back-and-forth over the 31 heel stitches.
Row 1 (RS): [Sl1, k1] 15x, k1, turn.
Row 2: Sl1, purl to end of row, turn.
Repeat Rows 1-2 an additional 15x.

Turn Heel

Row 1 (RS): Sl1, k16, SSK, k1, turn.
Row 2: Sl1, p4, p2tog, p1, turn.
Row 3: Sl1, knit to stitch before gap formed by previous row's turn, SSK, k1, turn.
Row 4: Sl1, purl to stitch before gap formed by previous row's turn, p2tog, p1, turn.
Repeat Rows 3-4 until one side stitch remains on either side of heel.

Next RS Row: Sl1, knit to stitch before gap formed by previous row's turn, SSK, turn.
Next WS Row: Sl1, purl to stitch before gap formed by previous row's turn, p2tog, turn. 17 heel stitches remain.

Shape Gusset

Knit across the 17 heel stitches. Working up the side of the heel flap with the same needle, pu 16 stitches. Work instep stitches in *Lace Pattern for Foot* as follows (or from chart on p. 82):

Lace Pattern for Foot

(over 33 stitches and 8 rounds)
Round 1: SSK, *k3, YO, k2tog, YO, k3, YO, SSK, YO, k3**, S2KP, repeat from * to **, k2tog.
Round 2: Knit.
Round 3: SSK, *[k2, YO] 2x, k2tog, k1, SSK, [YO, k2] 2x**, S2KP, repeat from * to **, k2tog.

Round 4: Knit.
Round 5: SSK, *k1, YO, k3, YO, k2tog, k1, SSK, YO, k3, YO, k1**, S2KP, repeat from * to **, k2tog.
Round 6: Knit.
Round 7: SSK, *YO, k3, YO, SSK, YO, S2KP, YO, k2tog, YO, k3, YO**, S2KP, repeat from * to **, k2tog.
Round 8: Knit.

Working down the other side of the heel flap with an empty dpn or empty end of second circular needle, pu 16 stitches. 49 heel stitches.

If using dpns, knit the first 8 stitches from the second heel needle onto the first so there are approximately an even number of heel stitches on each needle.

To get back to the beginning of the round, knit to the last 3 heel stitches, k2tog, k1. 48 heel stitches.

Round 1: Work instep stitches in Lace Pattern for Foot as established; k1, SSK, knit to end of heel stitches.
Round 2: Work instep stitches in Lace Pattern for Foot as established; knit to last 3 heel stitches, k2tog, k1.
Repeat Rounds 1-2 an additional 6x, then work Round 1 once more. 33 heel stitches, 66 total stitches.

Foot

Continue to work instep stitches in Lace Pattern for Foot as established and heel stitches in stockinette stitch until foot from start of heel turn to needles measures approximately 2" less than desired finished bottom-of-foot length, ending with Round 8 of pattern.

Toe

Round 1: Knit.
Round 2: *SSK, k14, pm, SSK, k15, pm; repeat from *. 62 stitches.
Round 3: Knit.
Round 4: *SSK, knit to marker; repeat from * an additional 3x. 58 stitches.
Repeat Rounds 3-4 an additional 9x, stopping one stitch before end of round on last working of Round 4, slip first instep stitch to end of heel needle, k2tog. 21 stitches.

Slip first heel stitch to end of adjacent instep needle. Remove markers.

Next Round: K3, k2tog, k4, k2tog, [k3, k2tog] 2x. 17 stitches.
Next Round: K2, k2tog, k3, k2tog, [k2, k2tog] 2x. 13 stitches.
Next Round: K1, k2tog, k2, k2tog, [k1, k2tog] 2x. 9 stitches.
Next Round: K2tog, k1, [k2tog] 3x. 5 stitches.

Cut yarn, leaving a 14-16" tail. With yarn needle, thread tail through remaining five stitches and pull tight. Weave in tail on WS of work to secure.

Finishing

Weave in any remaining ends, dampen socks and lay flat to block or use sock blockers.

Lace Pattern for Leg

Lace Pattern for Foot

knit
O YO
λ SSK
⋏ k2tog
⋀ S2KP

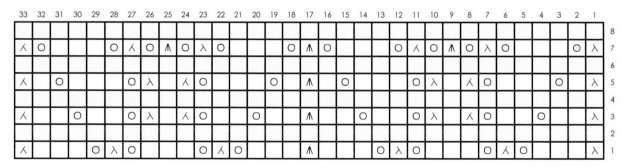

Flavorful Yarns

Materials:

Approximately 400 yards of fingering-weight yarn. *Sample uses Mountain Colors Crazyfoot (90% superwash merino, 10% nylon) in 'Northwind'.*

US1 (2.25mm) needles or size needed to obtain gauge

Yarn needle, cable needle

Gauge:

8-1/2 stitches/12 rounds per inch in stockinette stitch

Size:

Foot circumference = approximately 8"

Deux Tourbillions

Designer's Notes:

Tourbillion is another word for whirlpool, which perfectly reflects my inspiration for these vortex-like socks in a gorgeous blue color palette.

This was my first attempt at working with a spiraling stitch pattern, and I was delighted with how it turned out. Instead of the complicated mess I'd feared, spiraling the motif around the leg was quite simple. Once I let the stitch pattern off its leash and allowed it to run, it took care of itself very nicely.

After the first sock was complete, I opted for a mirror-image second sock to make both the knitting and the visual impact of the pair more interesting.

These are admittedly my favorite socks from the entire book (I'm considering making myself a second pair, something I almost never do). I hope you enjoy them as much as I did!

This was the June 2011 Indie Socks CSK featured pattern.

Right Sock
Leg

Cast on 72 stitches and divide them over dpns or circular needles as follows:

- If using dpns, place 24 stitches each on needles 1 and 3, and 12 stitches each on needles 2 and 4.
- If using circular needle(s), place 36 stitches on each needle.

The first 36 stitches of the round are the instep stitches and the last 36 stitches are the heel stitches. Join stitches into round being careful not to twist.

Round 1: *P3, k3; repeat from * to end of round.
Repeat Round 1 an additional 9x.

Begin working *Right Leg Pattern* as follows (or from chart) across all stitches:

Right Leg Pattern

(over a multiple of 12 stitches and 6 rounds)
Round 1: *YO, k5, YO, k2, k3tog, k2; repeat from * to end of round.
Round 2: Knit.
Round 3: *YO, k1, YO, k2, SSK, k3, k2tog, k2; repeat from * to end of round.
Round 4: Knit.
Round 5: *YO, k3, YO, k2, SSK, k1, k2tog, k2; repeat from * to end of round.
Round 6: Knit.

12	11	10	9	8	7	6	5	4	3	2	1	
												6
			k3tog		SSK		YO				YO	5
												4
			k3tog			SSK			YO		YO	3
												2
			k3tog		YO						YO	1

Symbol	Meaning
□	knit
人	k3tog
λ	SSK
人	k2tog
O	YO

Repeat Rounds 1-6 a total of 11x. Work across instep stitches in Round 1 of Right Instep Pattern as follows (or from chart on p. 89):

Right Instep Pattern

(over 36 stitches and 24 rounds)
Round 1: [K5, YO, k2, k3tog, k2, YO] 3x.
Round 2 (and all even-numbered rounds): Knit.
Round 3: [YO, k2, SSK, k3, k2tog, k2, YO, k1] 3x.
Round 5: K1, [YO, k2, SSK, k1, k2tog, k2, YO, k3] 2x, YO, k2, SSK, k1, k2tog, k2, YO, k2.
Round 7: K2, [YO, k2, k3tog, k2, YO, k5] 2x, YO, k2, k3tog, k2, YO, k3.
Round 9: K4, [k2tog, k2, YO, k1, YO, k2, SSK, k3] 2x, k2tog, k2, [YO, k1] twice, k2tog.

Round 11: K3, [k2tog, k2, YO, k3, YO, k2, SSK, k1] 2x, k2tog, k2, YO, k3, YO, k2tog.
Round 13: K2, k2tog, [k2, YO, k5, YO, k2, k3tog] 2x, k2, YO, k6.
Round 15: K1, [k2tog, k2, YO, k1, YO, k2, SSK, k3] 2x, k2tog, k2, YO, k1, YO, k2, SSK, k2.
Round 17: [K2tog, k2, YO, k3, YO, k2, SSK, k1] 3x.
Round 19: SSK, k1, [YO, k5, YO, k2, k3tog, k2] 2x, YO, k5, YO, k2, k2tog.
Round 21: SSK, [YO, k1, YO, k2, SSK, k3, k2tog, k2] 2x, YO, k1, YO, k2, SSK, k3, k2tog, m1.
Round 23: K4, [YO, k2, SSK, k1, k2tog, k2, YO, k3] 2x, YO, k2, SSK, k1, k2tog, k1, m1.

Heel Flap

The heel flap will now be worked back-and-forth over the 36 heel stitches.

Row 1 (RS): [Sl1, k1] 18x, turn.
Row 2: Sl1, purl to end of row, turn.
Repeat Rows 1-2 an additional 15x.

Turn Heel

Row 1 (RS): Sl1, k22, SSK, turn.
Row 2: Sl1, p10, p2tog, turn.
Row 3: Sl1, k10, SSK, turn.
Row 4: Repeat Row 2.
Repeat Rows 3-4 until all heel flap stitches have been worked. 12 heel stitches remain.

Shape Gusset

Knit across the 12 heel stitches. Working up the side of the heel flap with the same needle, pu 16 stitches. Work instep stitches in Round 2 of instep pattern. Working down the other side of the heel flap with an empty dpn or empty end of second circular needle, pu 16 stitches. 44 heel stitches.

If using dpns, knit the first 6 stitches from the second heel needle onto the first so there are an equal number of heel stitches on each needle.

To get back to the beginning of the round, knit to the end of the heel stitches.

Round 1: Work instep stitches in next round of instep pattern; knit to last 3 heel stitches, k2tog, k1.
Round 2: Work instep stitches in next round of instep pattern; k1, SSK, knit to end of heel stitches.
Repeat Rounds 1-2 an additional 3x. 36 heel stitches, 72 total stitches.

Foot

Continue to work instep stitches in pattern as established and heel stitches in stockinette stitch until foot from start of heel turn to needles measures approximately 2" less than desired finished bottom-of-foot length.

Toe

Round 1: *K1, SSK, knit to last 3 instep stitches, k2tog, k1; repeat from * across heel stitches.
Round 2: Knit.

Repeat Rounds 1-2 an additional 10x. 28 stitches. Then, repeat Round 1 only an additional 3x. 16 stitches.

Cut yarn, leaving a 14-16" tail. Graft toe closed using Kitchener Stitch.

Finishing

Weave in any remaining ends, dampen socks and lay flat to block or use sock blockers.

Left Sock
Leg

Cast on 72 stitches and divide them over dpns or circular needles as for Right Sock. Join stitches into round being careful not to twist.

Round 1: *K3, p3; repeat from * to end of round.
Repeat Round 1 an additional 9x.

Begin working *Left Leg Pattern* as follows (or from chart) across all stitches:

Left Leg Pattern

(over a multiple of 12 stitches and 6 rounds)
Round 1: *K2, SK2P, k2, YO, k5, YO; repeat from * to end of round.
Round 2: Knit.
Round 3: *K2, SSK, k3, k2tog, k2, YO, k1, YO; repeat from * to end of round.
Round 4: Knit.
Round 5: *K2, SSK, k1, k2tog, k2, YO, k3, YO; repeat from * to end of round.
Round 6: Knit.

	knit
λ	SK2P
λ	SSK
⋏	k2tog
O	YO

Repeat Rounds 1-6 a total of 11x. Work across instep stitches in Round 1 of Left Instep Pattern as follows (or from chart on p. 90), then work rest of sock as for Right Sock, starting with Heel Flap.

Left Instep Pattern

(over 36 stitches and 24 rounds)

Round 1: [YO, k2, SK2P, k2, YO, k5] 3x.

Round 2 (and all even-numbered rounds): Knit.

Round 3: [K1, YO, k2, SSK, k3, k2tog, k2, YO] 3x.

Round 5: K2, [YO, k2, SSK, k1, k2tog, k2, YO, k3] 2x, YO, k2, SSK, k1, k2tog, k2, YO, k1.

Round 7: K3, [YO, k2, SK2P, k2, YO, k5] 2x, YO, k2, SK2P, k2, YO, k2.

Round 9: SSK, k1, [YO, k1, YO, k2, SSK, k3, k2tog, k2] 2x, YO, k1, YO, k2, SSK, k4.

Round 11: SSK, [YO, k3, YO, k2, SSK, k1, k2tog, k2] 2x, YO, k3, YO, k2, SSK, k3.

Round 13: K6, [YO, k2, SK2P, k2, YO, k5] 2x, YO, k2, SSK, k2.

Round 15: K2, [k2tog, k2, YO, k1, YO, k2, SSK, k3] 2x, k2tog, k2, YO, k1, YO, k2, SSK, k1.

Round 17: [K1, k2tog, k2, YO, k3, YO, k2, SSK] 3x.

Round 19: SSK, [k2, YO, k5, YO, k2, SK2P] 2x, k2, YO, k5, YO, k1, k2tog.

Round 21: M1, [SSK, k3, k2tog, k2, YO, k1, YO, k2] 2x, SSK, k3, k2tog, k2, YO, k1, YO, k2tog.

Round 23: M1, k1, [SSK, k1, k2tog, k2, YO, k3, YO, k2] 2x, SSK, k1, k2tog, k2, YO, k4.

Right Instep Pattern

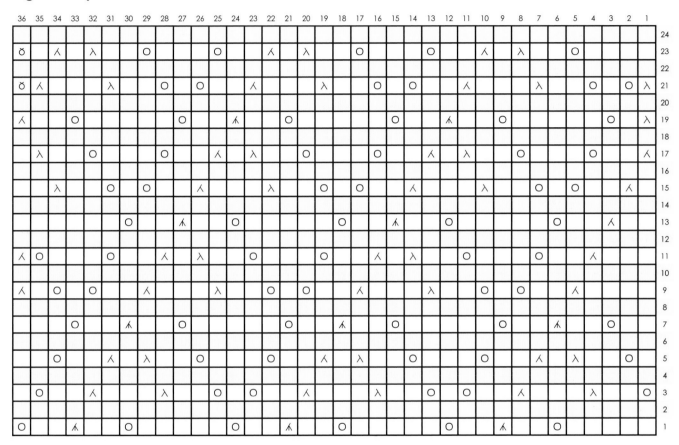

	knit
人	k3tog
λ	SSK
人	k2tog
O	YO
ð	m1

Left Instep Pattern

Column numbers (left to right): 36 35 34 33 32 31 30 29 28 27 26 25 24 23 22 21 20 19 18 17 16 15 14 13 12 11 10 9 8 7 6 5 4 3 2 1

Row	36	35	34	33	32	31	30	29	28	27	26	25	24	23	22	21	20	19	18	17	16	15	14	13	12	11	10	9	8	7	6	5	4	3	2	1
24																																				
23					O		人		λ				O				O			人		λ			O			O				人		λ		ð
22																																				
21	人	O		O			人			λ				O	O			人				λ			O	O				人				λ		ð
20																																				
19	人		O					O				λ		O				O					人			O						O				λ
18																																				
17	λ		O				O			人	λ			O				O				人	λ			O					O				人	
16																																				
15		λ			O		O			人				λ			O	O			人			λ		O	O				人					
14																																				
13			λ			O					O			人			O				O		人			O										
12																																				
11				λ		O				O				人	λ		O				O		人	λ		O								O		λ
10																																				
9						λ		O		O			人			λ		O	O			人		λ		O		O								λ
8																																				
7			O			人		O					人		O			人		O								O		人			O			
6																																				
5		O			人	λ			O				O			人	λ			O					O			人	λ			O				
4																																				
3	O		人			λ			O	O			人				λ			O	O		人			λ						O				
2																																				
1						O		人		O							O		人		O						O		人		O					O

Legend

Symbol	Meaning
□	knit
人	SK2P
λ	SSK
𝅻	k2tog
O	YO
ð	m1

Socks need to be knit more firmly than other garments because they receive an incredible amount of abuse inside your shoes or, alternately, being shuffled along rough floors while subjected to your entire body weight concentrated on a small area of fabric.

To keep your socks from wearing out instantly, you will want to knit them on smaller needles and with a tighter gauge than you would use for a sweater or scarf. This will also prevent the uncomfortable tendency of looser stitches to imprint themselves into the bottom of your foot.

In my experience, the best gauge for socks is somewhere between eight and ten stitches per inch, depending on how thick the yarn is (thicker yarn will have fewer stitches per inch while still giving a nice firm fabric).

For worsted or bulky-weight socks, you would use slightly larger needles, but I never recommend going over a US4 (3.5mm) needle even with very thick yarn. My first pair of socks were some simple worsted-weight anklets knit on US5 (3.75mm) needles, and I wore holes through the balls of the feet in just a few short months. They are now relegated to my "museum drawer".

Remember that the needle size printed in any pattern is only a suggestion and you may not be able to "just start knitting" without checking your gauge.

Tips & Tricks: Gauge & Knitted Fabric for Socks

Materials:

Approximately 400 yards of fingering-weight yarn. *Sample uses Artyarns Cashmere Sock Yarn (67% cashmere, 25% wool, 8% nylon) in Color #168.*

US1-1/2 (2.5mm) needles or size needed to obtain gauge

Yarn needle

Gauge:

8 stitches/12 rounds per inch in stockinette stitch

Size:

Foot circumference = approximately 8"

Gelato

Designer's Notes:

This luscious cashmere sock yarn from indie dyeing powerhouse Artyarns is fantastically soft yet strong, thanks to an interlaced reinforcing strand of wool and nylon. Since the hues of this colorway are nice and light, I opted for an allover diamond pattern that works nicely with the diffuse striping of the yarn.

This pattern, like Deux Tourbillions on p. 84, features a series of diagonal ribs running around the leg. When knitting these socks, after turning the heel and working up the leg, you'll notice that the beginning of the round spirals around the sock as you knit up. This allows for an uninterrupted pattern up the leg, without the usual beginning of round jog. I find these spiraling sock legs to be great fun!

The soft, cushy nature of this yarn makes me think of slippers, so I finished these socks off with a casual roll top. You won't want to wear them on bare floors, but they will keep your feet toasty inside your shoes or under the covers!

Toe

Using Judy's Magic Cast-On or your favorite toe-up cast on, cast on 7 instep stitches and 7 heel stitches (14 total stitches), dividing them over your selected needles.

Round 1: Knit.
Round 2: *K-fb, knit to last 2 instep stitches, k-fb, k1; repeat from * across heel stitches. 18 stitches.
Repeat Round 2 only an additional 2x. 26 stitches. Then, repeat Rounds 1-2 an additional 8x. 58 stitches, 29 instep and 29 heel. Knit one round even.

Next Round: K-fb, knit to last 2 instep stitches, k-fb, k1; knit to end of heel stitches. 60 stitches, 31 instep and 29 heel.

Foot

Begin working *Instep Pattern* as follows (or from chart on p. 96) across the instep stitches. Continue working heel stitches in stockinette stitch.

Instep Pattern

(over 31 stitches and 20 rounds)
Round 1 (and all odd-numbered rounds): Knit.
Round 2: K3, [k2tog, YO, k1, YO, SSK, k5] 2x, k2tog, YO, k1, YO, SSK, k3.
Round 4: K2, [k2tog, YO, k3, YO, SSK, k3] 2x, k2tog, YO, k3, YO, SSK, k2.

Round 6: *K1, [k2tog, YO] 2x, k1, [YO, SSK] 2x; repeat from * to last instep stitch, k1.
Round 8: [K2tog, YO, k1] 2x, [YO, SSK, k1, YO, SK2P, YO, k1, k2tog, YO, k1] twice, YO, SSK, k1, YO, SSK.
Round 10: [YO, SSK, k1, k2tog, YO, k1, YO, SSK, k2] 2x, YO, SSK, k1, k2tog, YO, k1, YO, SSK, k1, k2tog, YO.
Round 12: [K1, YO, SSK, k5, k2tog, YO] 3x, k1.
Round 14: K2, [YO, SSK, k3, k2tog, YO, k3] 2x, YO, SSK, k3, k2tog, YO, k2.
Round 16: *K1, [YO, SSK] 2x, k1, [k2tog, YO] 2x; repeat from * to last instep stitch, k1.
Round 18: [K1, YO, SSK, k1, YO, SK2P, YO, k1, k2tog, YO] 3x, k1.
Round 20: [K1, YO, SSK, k2, YO, SSK, k1, k2tog, YO] 3x, k1.
Repeat Rounds 1-20 until foot measures approximately 2" less than desired finished foot length, ending with Round 7 of pattern.

Heel

Work across instep stitches in Round 8 of *Instep Pattern*. The heel turn will now be worked back-and-forth over the 29 heel stitches.

Shape Bottom of Heel

Row 1 (RS): K28, W&T.
Row 2 (WS): P27, W&T.
Row 3: Knit to stitch before wrapped stitch (do not knit any wrapped stitches), W&T.
Row 4: Purl to stitch before wrapped stitch (do not purl any wrapped stitches), W&T.
Repeat Rows 3-4 an additional 8x – there are now 10 wrapped stitches on either side of 9 unwrapped center stitches.

Shape Top of Heel

Row 1 (RS): Knit to first wrapped stitch (do not knit across any wrapped stitches), lift wrap RS, turn.
Row 2 (WS): Purl to first wrapped stitch (do not purl across any wrapped stitches), lift wrap WS, turn.
Row 3: Sl1, knit to next wrapped stitch (just past the stitch unwrapped on the previous RS row), lift wrap RS, turn.
Row 4: Sl1, purl to next wrapped stitch (just past the stitch unwrapped on the previous WS row), lift wrap WS, turn.
Repeat Rows 3-4 an additional 7x – a single wrapped stitch remains on either side of heel.

Next Row: Sl1, knit to last wrapped stitch, lift wrap RS but do not turn. You should be at the beginning of the instep stitches.
Next Round: Work instep stitches in Round 9 of *Instep Pattern*; lift wrap RS, knit to end of heel stitches.

Leg

Begin working all stitches in *Leg Pattern* as follows (or from chart on p. 96):

Note: When working the first round, work the first 3 pattern repeats/30 stitches on circular 1 or dpns 1 and 2, and the last 3 repeats/30 stitches on circular 2 or dpns 3 and 4. This will *happen naturally due to the placement of the YOs and does not require any rearranging of stitches.*

This will allow the pattern to spiral nicely around the leg and avoid having to move any stitches around to work the decreases. The beginning of round will slowly move around the leg as you work multiple repeats of the pattern.

Leg Pattern

(over multiple of 10 stitches and 10 rounds)

Round 1: *SSK, k1, k2tog, YO, k1, YO, SSK, k2, YO; repeat from * to end of round.

Round 2 *(and all even-numbered rounds)*: Knit.

Round 3: *SSK, k5, k2tog, YO, k1, YO; repeat from * to end of round.

Round 5: *SSK, k3, k2tog, YO, k3, YO.

Round 7: *SSK, k1, [k2tog, YO] 2x, k1, YO, SSK, YO; repeat from * to end of round.

Round 9: *SK2P, YO, k1, k2tog, YO, k1, YO, SSK, k1, YO; repeat from * to end of round.

Work in *Leg Pattern* until leg measures approximately 4-1/2" from top of heel (or 1/2" less than desired finished length).

Cuff

Knit 10 rounds.

Bind off all stitches loosely as follows: K1, *YO, k1, using tip of left needle, pass 2nd and 3rd stitch on right needle over 1st stitch on right needle (one stitch remains on right needle); repeat from * until all stitches are bound off. Fasten off.

Finishing

Weave in any remaining ends, dampen socks and lay flat to block or use sock blockers.

Instep Pattern

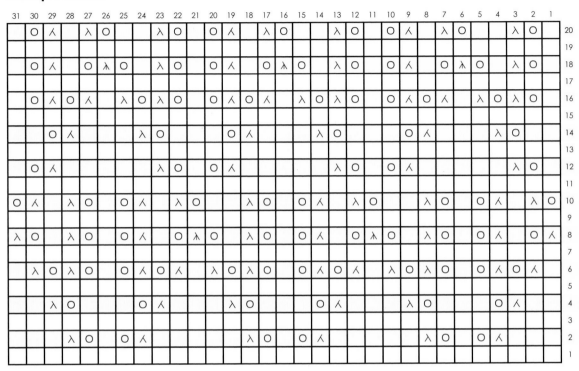

Leg Pattern

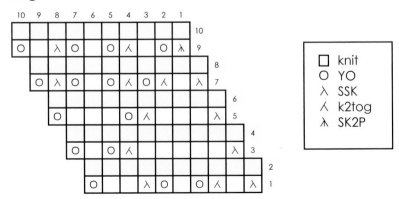

□	knit
O	YO
λ	SSK
⅄	k2tog
⋏	SK2P

Judy's Magic Cast-On is my go-to cast-on for toe-up socks. To work this cast-on, hold one needle horizontally and drape the yarn over it with the tail toward you, and the yarn going to ball (working yarn) away from you. You will need a 6-8" tail for the socks in this book. Give the yarn a half twist below the needle, so that the tail is now away from you and the working yarn is toward you (the reverse of a long-tail cast-on).

Hold a second needle just below the needle with the yarn loop already on it. The yarn loop will be the first stitch cast on to the top needle. Tent the yarn strands over the thumb and index finger of your left hand as if doing a long-tail cast-on. The tail will wrap around your index finger and the working yarn will rest on your thumb.

Cast the first stitch onto the bottom needle by bringing both needles up and around the yarn tail on your index finger.

The yarn will wrap around the bottom of the empty second needle from back to front as for a YO. Slip the yarn tail between the needles to complete the loop around the bottom needle. There is now one stitch on each needle.

Cast the next stitch onto the top needle by bringing both needles down and around the working yarn on your thumb. The yarn will wrap around the top of the top needle from back to front. Slip the working yarn between the needles to complete the loop around the top needle.

Repeat these last two movements, casting a stitch onto the bottom needle, then the top needle, until there are the desired number of stitches on each needle.

Rotate needles so that the yarn tail and working yarn are on your right. The working yarn should be coming off the bottom needle and the yarn tail off the top needle.

Judy's Magic Cast-On

You will begin working across the stitches on the top needle. Make sure to capture the yarn tail by placing it between the top needle and the working yarn as you knit the first stitch. You can pull the yarn tail to firm up any looseness at the beginning of this round.

For more on Judy's Magic Cast-On, visit www.persistentillusion.com and click on the Techniques tab.

Pagewood Farm

HAND DYED
SOCK YARN

Hand dyed in small batches in the USA

ALYESKA

Materials:

Approximately 400 yards of fingering-weight yarn. *Sample uses Pagewood Farm Alyeska (80% superwash merino wool) in 'Lavender Fields'.*

US1 (2.25mm) needles or size needed to obtain gauge

Yarn needle

Gauge:

8 stitches/11 rounds per inch in stockinette stitch

Size:

Foot circumference = approximately 7-1/2"

Rippleside

Designer's Notes:

This resplendent green and blue colorway immediately brought to mind the lakes and rivers of my home state, Minnesota.

Growing up, I thought it was totally normal to run into a lake every other mile. The tiny town where I grew up didn't have a public swimming pool, so we spent summers swimming in the various lakes and rivers nearby. I have so many fond memories of cool, blue-green lake water dotted with lily pads and duckweed.

These socks were inspired by cool lake breezes and named after my elementary school, which was on the banks of the Ripple River. I found a stitch pattern that reminds me of the ripples sent across the surface of the water by a gust of wind, and since these gusts head every which way, I mirrored the design down the back of the leg, and then reversed it on the second sock.

This pattern does tend to bias, but a good blocking (or putting the socks on your feet) should mitigate any strange slanting that goes on.

Toe

Using Judy's Magic Cast-On or your favorite toe-up cast on, cast on 9 instep stitches and 9 heel stitches (18 total stitches), dividing them over your selected needles.

Round 1: Knit.
Round 2: *K-fb, knit to last 2 instep stitches, k-fb, k1; repeat from * across heel stitches. 22 stitches.
Repeat Round 2 only an additional 2x. 30 stitches. Then, repeat Rounds 1-2 an additional 7x. 58 stitches, 29 instep and 29 heel. Knit one round even.

Next Round: K-fb, knit to last 2 instep stitches, k-fb, k1; knit to end of heel stitches. 60 stitches, 31 instep and 29 heel.
Next Round: Knit.

Foot

Begin working *Instep Pattern* Rounds 1-12 for the appropriate foot as follows (or from charts on p. 102) across the instep stitches. Continue working heel stitches in stockinette stitch.

Left Instep Pattern
(over 31 stitches and 12 rounds)
Round 1: [K1, p1, k5, k2tog, YO, p1] 3x, k1.
Round 2 (and all even-numbered rounds): P2, [k7, p3] 2x, k7, p2.

Round 3: [K1, p1, k4, k2tog, k1, YO, p1] 3x, k1.
Round 5: [K1, p1, k3, k2tog, k2, YO, p1] 3x, k1.
Round 7: [K1, p1, k2, k2tog, k3, YO, p1] 3x, k1.
Round 9: [K1, p1, k1, k2tog, k4, YO, p1] 3x, k1.
Round 11: [K1, p1, k2tog, k5, YO, p1] 3x, k1.

Right Instep Pattern
(over 31 stitches and 12 rounds)
Round 1: [K1, p1, YO, SSK, k5, p1] 3x, k1.
Round 2 (and all even-numbered rounds): P2, [k7, p3] 2x, k7, p2.
Round 3: [K1, p1, YO, k1, SSK, k4, p1] 3x, k1.
Round 5: [K1, p1, YO, k2, SSK, k3, p1] 3x, k1.
Round 7: [K1, p1, YO, k3, SSK, k2, p1] 3x, k1.
Round 9: [K1, p1, YO, k4, SSK, k1, p1] 3x, k1.
Round 11: [K1, p1, YO, k5, SSK, p1] 3x, k1.

Repeat Rounds 1-12 of *Instep Pattern* until foot measures approximately 4-1/4" less than desired finished foot length.

Gusset

Round 1: Work instep stitches in *Instep Pattern* as established; k-fb in first heel stitch, knit to last 2 heel stitches, k-fb, k1.
Round 2: Work instep stitches in *Instep Pattern* as established; knit across all heel stitches.
Repeat Rounds 1-2 an additional 13x, then work Round 1 once more. 59 heel stitches.

Turn Heel

Work across instep stitches in pattern. The heel turn will be worked back-and-forth over the 59 heel stitches.
Row 1 (RS): K43, W&T.
Row 2 (WS): P27, W&T.
Row 3: Knit to stitch before wrapped stitch (do not knit any wrapped stitches), W&T.
Row 4: Purl to stitch before wrapped stitch (do not purl any wrapped stitches), W&T.
Repeat Rows 3-4 an additional 7x – there are now 9 wrapped stitches on either side of 11 unwrapped center stitches. Knit to end of heel stitches, lifting wraps RS as they are encountered, then work across instep stitches in pattern.

Heel Flap

Work the heel flap back and forth.
Row 1 (RS): K43, lifting remaining wraps RS as you encounter them, SSK, turn.
Row 2 (WS): Sl1 wyif, [p1, sl1-wyib] 13x, p1, p2tog, turn.

Row 3: Sl1, k27, SSK, turn.

Row 4: Sl1-wyif, [sl1-wyib, p1] 13x, sl1-wyib, p2tog, turn.

Row 5: Repeat Row 3.

Repeat Rows 2-5 an additional 6x. Do not turn after final working of Row 5. As you do this, you are slowly working up the edge of the gusset and forming the heel flap as you go. At the end, you are left with 61 stitches, 31 instep and 30 heel.

Next Round: Work across instep stitches in pattern; k2tog, knit to end of heel stitches. 60 stitches, 31 instep and 29 heel.

Leg

Continue to work the instep stitches in *Instep Pattern* as established. Begin working the heel stitches in *Back Leg Pattern* Rounds 1-12 for the appropriate foot as follows (or from charts on p. 103). Begin the *Back Leg Pattern* on the same round as the *Instep Pattern* so that the design will line up around the leg.

Left Back Leg Pattern

(over 29 stitches and 12 rounds)

Round 1: [P1, YO, SSK, k5, p1, k1] 2x, p1, YO, SSK, k5, p1.

Round 2 (and all even-numbered rounds): P1, [k7, p3] 2x, k7, p1.

Round 3: [P1, YO, k1, SSK, k4, p1, k1] 2x, p1, YO, k1, SSK, k4, p1.

Round 5: [P1, YO, k2, SSK, k3, p1, k1] 2x, p1, YO, k2, SSK, k3, p1.

Round 7: [P1, YO, k3, SSK, k2, p1, k1] 2x, p1, YO, k3, SSK, k2, p1.

Round 9: [P1, YO, k4, SSK, k1, p1, k1] 2x, p1, YO, k4, SSK, k1, p1.

Round 11: [P1, YO, k5, SSK, p1, k1] 2x, p1, YO, k5, SSK, p1.

Right Back Leg Pattern

(over 29 stitches and 12 rounds)

Round 1: [P1, k5, k2tog, YO, p1, k1] 2x, p1, k5, k2tog, YO, p1.

Round 2 (and all even-numbered rounds): P1, [k7, p3] 2x, k7, p1.

Round 3: [P1, k4, k2tog, k1, YO, p1, k1] 2x, p1, k4, k2tog, k1, YO, p1.

Round 5: [P1, k3, k2tog, k2, YO, p1, k1] 2x, p1, k3, k2tog, k2, YO, p1.

Round 7: [P1, k2, k2tog, k3, YO, p1, k1] 2x, p1, k2, k2tog, k3, YO, p1.

Round 9: [P1, k1, k2tog, k4, YO, p1, k1] 2x, p1, k1, k2tog, k4, YO, p1.

Round 11: [P1, k2tog, k5, YO, p1, k1] 2x, p1, k2tog, k5, YO, p1.

Work in pattern until leg measures approximately 4" from top of heel flap or 1" less than desired finished leg length.

Cuff

Work cuff in [k1, p1] rib for 1".

Bind off all stitches loosely as follows: K1, *YO, k1, using tip of left needle, pass 2nd and 3rd stitch on right needle over 1st stitch on right needle (one stitch remains on right needle); repeat from * until all stitches are bound off. Fasten off.

Finishing

Weave in any remaining ends, dampen socks and lay flat to block or use sock blockers.

Left Instep Pattern

Row	31	30	29	28	27	26	25	24	23	22	21	20	19	18	17	16	15	14	13	12	11	10	9	8	7	6	5	4	3	2	1
12	•	•								•	•	•								•	•	•								•	•
11		•	O						∧	•		•	O						∧	•		•	O						∧	•	
10	•	•								•	•	•								•	•	•								•	•
9		•	O					∧		•		•	O					∧		•		•	O					∧		•	
8	•	•								•	•	•								•	•	•								•	•
7		•	O				∧			•		•	O				∧			•		•	O				∧			•	
6	•	•								•	•	•								•	•	•								•	•
5		•	O			∧				•		•	O			∧				•		•	O			∧				•	
4	•	•								•	•	•								•	•	•								•	•
3		•	O		∧					•		•	O		∧					•		•	O		∧					•	
2	•	•								•	•	•								•	•	•								•	•
1		•	O	∧						•		•	O	∧						•		•	O	∧						•	

Right Instep Pattern

Row	31	30	29	28	27	26	25	24	23	22	21	20	19	18	17	16	15	14	13	12	11	10	9	8	7	6	5	4	3	2	1
12	•	•								•	•	•								•	•	•								•	•
11		•	λ						O	•		•	λ						O	•		•	λ						O	•	
10	•	•								•	•	•								•	•	•								•	•
9		•		λ					O	•		•		λ					O	•		•		λ					O	•	
8	•	•								•	•	•								•	•	•								•	•
7		•			λ				O	•		•			λ				O	•		•			λ				O	•	
6	•	•								•	•	•								•	•	•								•	•
5		•				λ			O	•		•				λ			O	•		•				λ			O	•	
4	•	•								•	•	•								•	•	•								•	•
3		•					λ		O	•		•					λ		O	•		•					λ		O	•	
2	•	•								•	•	•								•	•	•								•	•
1		•						λ	O	•		•						λ	O	•		•						λ	O	•	

Legend:
- □ knit
- • purl
- O YO
- λ SSK
- ∧ k2tog

Left Back Leg Pattern

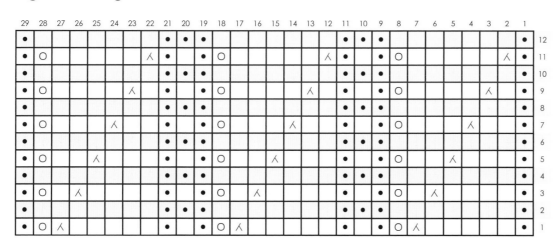

Right Back Leg Pattern

Legend:
- □ knit
- ● purl
- ○ YO
- λ SSK
- ⋏ k2tog

Materials:

Approximately 300 (370, 450) yards of fingering-weight yarn. *Samples use LavenderSheep Panda Wool Sock (46% bamboo, 43% wool, 5% nylon) in 'Owen' (child's socks) and 'Mountain Sunset' (adult socks).*

US1 (2.25mm) needles or size needed to obtain gauge

Yarn needle

Gauge:

9 stitches/12 rounds per inch in stockinette stitch

Size:

Foot circumference = approximately 6 (8-1/2, 11)"

Owenburger

Designer's Notes:

When I first mentioned the Indie Socks book concept to my friend Yvonne, the mastermind behind LavenderSheep, I noted that my son was expecting a pair of socks to be named after him (his sister had her namesake socks in my first book, *Toe-Up!*). Yvonne immediately leapt at the chance to design a custom colorway for my book, inspired by my fun-loving little boy.

The *Owen* colorway is a semi-solid consisting of stunning shades of my Owen's favorite color, blue. I opted to make an adult-sized pair for myself in another favorite LavenderSheep colorway, *Mountain Sunset*.

I opted to keep this sock simple and somewhat boyish with easy cable columns interrupted by occasional rounds of garter stitch. A fold-over cuff is inspired by manly work socks and the pattern is sized to fit the whole family. It can be worked either top-down or toe-up for ultimate flexibility.

This was the April 2011 Indie Socks CSK featured pattern.

Toe-Up Version

Using Judy's Magic Cast-On or your favorite toe-up cast on, cast on 6 (8, 10) instep stitches and 6 (8, 10) heel stitches (12, 16, 20 total stitches), dividing them over your selected needles.

Round 1: Knit.
Round 2: *K-fb, knit to last 2 instep stitches, k-fb, k1; repeat from * across heel stitches. 16 (20, 24) stitches.

Repeat Round 2 only an additional 2 (2, 3)x. 24 (28, 36) stitches. Then, repeat Rounds 1-2 an additional 9 (14, 18)x. 60 (84, 108), stitches, 30 (42, 54) instep and 30 (42, 54) heel.

Foot

Begin working instep stitches in *Stacked Cables Pattern* as follows (or from chart on p. 108) and heel stitches in stockinette stitch. Work until foot measures 1-3/4 (2-1/4, 3)" less than desired finished length from tip of toe.

Stacked Cables Pattern

(over 30(42, 54) stitches and 32 rounds)
Round 1: Purl.
Round 2: P1, [k4, p2] 4 (6, 8)x, k4, p1.
Round 3: P1, [C2B, C2F, p2, k4, p2] 2 (3, 4)x, C2B, C2F, p1.
Round 4: P1, [k4, p2] 4 (6, 8)x, k4, p1.

Round 5: P1, [C2F, C2B, p2, C4B, p2] 2 (3, 4)x, C2F, C2B, p1.
Round 6: P1, [k4, p2] 4 (6, 8)x, k4, p1.
Rounds 7-14: Repeat Rounds 3-6 twice.
Round 15: Purl.
Round 16: P1, [k4, p2] 4 (6, 8)x, k4, p1.
Rounds 17-18: Repeat Rounds 15-16.
Round 19: P1, [k4, p2, C2B, C2F, p2] 2 (3, 4)x, k4, p1.
Round 20: P1, [k4, p2] 4 (6, 8)x, k4, p1.
Round 21: P1, [C4B, p2, C2F, C2B, p2] 2 (3, 4)x, C4B, p1.
Round 22: P1, [k4, p2] 4 (6, 8)x, k4, p1.
Rounds 23-30: Repeat Rounds 19-22 twice.
Round 31: Purl.
Round 32: P1, [k4, p2] 4 (6, 8)x, k4, p1.

Heel

Work across instep stitches in pattern. The heel turn will now be worked back-and-forth over the 30 (42, 54) heel stitches.

Shape Bottom of Heel

Row 1 (RS): K29 (41, 53), W&T.
Row 2 (WS): P28 (40, 52), W&T.
Row 3: Knit to stitch before wrapped stitch (do not knit any wrapped stitches), W&T.
Row 4: Purl to stitch before wrapped stitch (do not purl any wrapped stitches), W&T.

Repeat Rows 3-4 an additional 8 (12, 16)x – there are now 10 (14, 18) wrapped stitches on either side of 10 (14, 18) unwrapped center stitches.

Shape Top of Heel

Row 1 (RS): Knit to first wrapped stitch (do not knit across any wrapped stitches), lift wrap RS, turn.
Row 2 (WS): Purl to first wrapped stitch (do not purl across any wrapped stitches), lift wrap WS, turn.
Row 3: Sl1, knit to next wrapped stitch (just past the stitch unwrapped on the previous RS row), lift wrap RS, turn.
Row 4: Sl1, purl to next wrapped stitch (just past the stitch unwrapped on the previous WS row), lift wrap WS, turn.

Repeat Rows 3-4 an additional 7 (11, 15)x – a single wrapped stitch remains on either side of heel.

Next Row: Sl1, knit to last wrapped stitch, lift wrap RS but do not turn. You should be at the beginning of the instep stitches.
Next Round: Work instep stitches in pattern as established; lift wrap RS, knit to end of heel stitches.

Leg

Begin working all stitches in *Stacked Cables Pattern* as established. Work even in pattern until leg measures approximately 3-1/2 (4-1/2, 5)" from top of heel, ending with Round 16 or 31 of pattern.

Cuff
Work in k1, p1 rib for 2 (2-1/2, 3)".

Bind off all stitches loosely as follows: K1, *YO, k1, using tip of left needle, pass 2nd and 3rd stitches on right needle over 1st stitch on right needle (one stitch remains on right needle); repeat from * until all stitches are bound off. Fasten off.

Finishing
Weave in any remaining ends, dampen socks and lay flat to block or use sock blockers.

Top-Down Version
Cast on 60 (84, 108) stitches and divide them over dpns or circular needles as follows:
- If using dpns, place 12 (18, 24) stitches on needle 1, 18 (24, 30) stitches on needle 2, 12 (18, 24) stitches on needle 3, and 18 (24, 30) stitches on needle 4.
- If using circular needle(s), place 30 (42, 54) stitches on each of needles 1 and 2.

The first 30 (42, 54) stitches of the round are the instep stitches and the last 30 (42, 54) stitches are the heel stitches.

Join stitches into round being careful not to twist.

Cuff
Work in k1, p1 rib for 2 (2-1/2, 3)".

Leg
Begin working all stitches in *Stacked Cables Pattern* as for toe-up sock. Work even in pattern until patterned portion of leg measures approximately 3-1/2 (4-1/2, 5)", ending with Round 16 or 31 of pattern.

Heel
Work as for toe-up sock (in this case, the Shape Bottom of Heel section will actually be the top of the heel and vice versa).

Foot
Continue working instep stitches in pattern as established and begin working heel stitches in stockinette stitch. Work until foot measures 1-1/2 (2, 2-1/2)" less than desired finished length, ending with Round 16 or 31 of pattern. If needed, work a few rounds of stockinette stitch to get foot to correct length.

Toe
Round 1: *K1, SSK, knit to last 3 instep stitches, k2tog, k1; repeat from *

across heel stitches. 56 (80, 104) stitches.
Round 2: Knit.
Repeat Rounds 1-2 an additional 8 (13, 17)x. 24 (28, 36) stitches. Then, repeat Round 1 only an additional 3 (3, 4)x. 12 (16, 20) stitches.

Graft toe closed using Kitchener stitch.

Finishing
Finish as for toe-up sock.

Stacked Cables Pattern

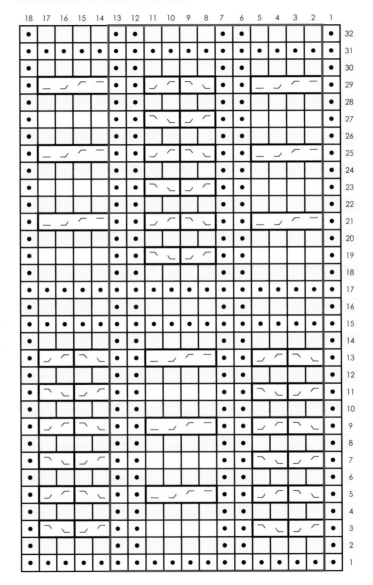

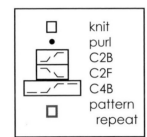

knit
purl
C2B
C2F
C4B
pattern repeat

I know many of you will hate me for saying this, but I'll say it anyway – SWATCHING IS YOUR FRIEND. I'll say it a thousand times, because it really is true. I don't always like to swatch myself (and I'll often just tell myself that my sock cuff/toe IS my swatch), but it really can end up saving you a lot of wasted time and frustration.

When I begin a new project, I start out with a small swatch equivalent to half of my sock. I knit it flat, acknowledging that the colors in a variegated yarn will fall differently in a small flat swatch than in a full-size round swatch.

Once I work a pattern repeat or two, I can easily see if the stitch pattern is going to work with the yarn or not. If not, I don't have the pain of ripping out an entire cuff (including ribbing) or foot (including the toe).

If I think the pattern will be successful, I start knitting the toe or cuff, knowing that things still may take a turn for the worse when I start working over twice as many stitches. This happens very rarely, however, so I give it an 80% chance of success if I like the way the small swatch looks.

If you're comparing a few different patterns, it's a great exercise to make a small swatch of each and line them up next to each other. You might be surprised at which one looks the best.

There have been many times in my design career when I've had a stitch that's working well enough, but not great, and I've found a much better option by doing these little swatches and comparing them.

I often start out with a stitch that I think is going to look just fabulous, and my swatch looks like something the cat yakked up. I switch to a stitch I'm not as in love with, and it sings. You just don't always know how it's going to turn out until you give it a try.

That said, there are a few fabric characteristics that tend to work better with variegated yarns, and they generally include one or more of the following – diagonal or wave-like movement (i.e. feather and fan), slipped stitches, purl stitches, garter ridges and/or sharp textural details.

You'll notice that the patterns in the "Spicy Yarns" section of the book use many of these elements to create an interesting design that is not totally overshadowed by the coloration of the yarn. It's not an easy job!

Tips & Tricks: Taming Variegated Yarns

Creatively
Dyed Yarn

creativelydyedyarn.com

Steele

Color: String Thing

100% su
mer

510 yard
1 - 3

Materials:

Approximately 400-450 yards of fingering-weight yarn. *Sample uses Creatively Dyed Steele (100% superwash merino) in 'String Thing'.*

US1 (2.25mm) needles or size needed to obtain gauge

Yarn needle, cable needle

Gauge:

8 stitches/11 rounds per inch in stockinette stitch
10 stitches/13 rounds per inch in diamond pattern

Size:

Foot circumference = approximately 8"

Nuppy Diamonds

Designer's Notes:

Dianne's yarns are always a fun challenge to design with. Her vivid use of splashes of color stands on its own, and the challenge is to find a stitch pattern that will work with the playfulness of the yarn rather than muddying it.

After several false starts, I developed this simple design of traveling stitch diamonds. Since plain diamonds felt a little bit too...plain, I alternated columns of reverse-stockinette diamonds and stockinette diamonds with a nupp in the center of each (nupps because I wanted the pattern to extend down the foot, and that many bobbles would be too bumpy inside a shoe).

A linen stitch heel echoes the horizontal strands of the nupps and plays with the fun colors of the yarn one last time. The twisted stitch pattern really pulls in, so don't be alarmed by the large stitch count. Fortunately, Steele comes in generous 150g skeins, making socks like these possible without fear of running short.

This was the November 2010 Indie Socks CSK featured pattern.

Special Abbreviations and Techniques for This Pattern

nupp: To work nupp, insert right needle between 2nd and 3rd stitches on left needle from front to back. Wrap working yarn clockwise around tip of right needle and draw up a loop. Place this loop onto the left needle and knit it without twisting. Sl2, then pass stitch knitted in loop over the two slipped stitches.

Leg

Cast on 80 stitches and divide them over dpns or circular needles as follows:

- If using dpns, place 20 stitches on each needle.
- If using circular needle(s), place 40 stitches on each needle.

The first 40 stitches of the round are the instep stitches and the last 40 stitches are the heel stitches. Join stitches into round being careful not to twist.

Round 1: K1, *p3, k2; repeat from * to last 4 stitches of round, p3, k1.
Repeat Round 1 an additional 7x.

Begin working *Twisted Diamond Pattern* as follows (or from chart) across all stitches:

Twisted Diamond Pattern

(over a multiple of 10 stitches and 10 rounds)

Round 1: P4, *k-tbl 2x, p8; repeat from * to last 6 stitches, k-tbl 2x, p4.

Round 2: P3, *C2B, C2F, p6; repeat from * to last 7 stitches, C2B, C2F, p3.

Round 3: P2, *C2B, k2, C2F, p4; repeat from * to last 8 stitches, C2B, k2, C2F, p2.

Round 4: P1, *C2B, k4, C2F, p2; repeat from * to last 9 stitches, C2B, k4, C2F, p1.

Round 5: *C2B, k6, C2F; repeat from * to end.

Round 6: K-tbl, *k3, nupp, k3, k-tbl 2x; repeat from * to last 9 stitches, k3, nupp, k3, k-tbl.

Round 7: *T2F, k6, T2B; repeat from * to end.

Round 8: P1, *T2F, k4, T2B, p2; repeat from * to last 9 stitches, T2F, k4, T2B, p1.

Round 9: P2, *T2F, k2, T2B, p4; repeat from * to last 8 stitches, T2F, k2, T2B, p2.

Round 10: P3, *T2F, T2B, p6; repeat from * to last 7 stitches, T2F, T2B, p3.

Repeat Rounds 1-10 until leg measures approximately 5" from start (or desired length to top of heel flap), ending with Round 10 of pattern.

Twisted Diamond Pattern

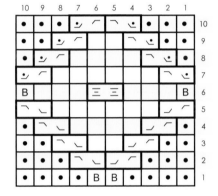

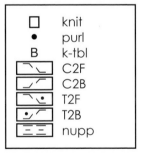

Heel Flap

Work across instep stitches in pattern. The heel flap will then be worked back-and-forth over the 40 heel stitches.

Row 1 (RS): Sl1, [k1, sl1-wyif] 19x, k1, turn.
Row 2: Sl1, purl to end of row, turn.
Row 3: Sl1, [sl1-wyif, k1] 19x, k1, turn.
Row 4: Sl1, purl to end of row, turn.

Repeat Rows 1-4 an additional 7x.

Turn Heel

Row 1 (RS): Sl1, k20, SSK, k1, turn.
Row 2: Sl1, p3, p2tog, p1, turn.
Row 3: Sl1, knit to stitch before gap formed by previous row's turn, SSK, k1, turn.
Row 4: Sl1, purl to stitch before gap formed by previous row's turn, p2tog, p1, turn.
Repeat Rows 3-4 until all heel flap stitches have been worked. 22 heel stitches remain.

Shape Gusset

Knit across the 22 heel stitches. Working up the side of the heel flap with the same needle, pu 16 stitches. Work instep stitches in pattern as established. Working down the other side of the heel flap with an empty dpn or empty end of second circular needle, pu 16 stitches. 54 heel stitches.

If using dpns, knit the first 11 stitches from the second heel needle onto the first so there are an equal number of heel stitches on each needle.

To get back to the beginning of the round, knit to the last 3 heel stitches, k2tog, k1. 53 heel stitches.

Round 1: Work instep stitches in pattern as established; k1, SSK, knit to end of heel stitches.
Round 2: Work instep stitches in pattern as established; knit to last 3 heel stitches, k2tog, k1.
Repeat Rounds 1-2 an additional 9x, then work Round 1 once more. 32 heel stitches, 72 total stitches.

Foot

Continue to work instep stitches in pattern as established and heel stitches in stockinette stitch until foot from start of heel turn to needles measures approximately 2" less than desired finished bottom-of-foot length, ending with Round 6 of pattern.

Next Round: [SSK, k6, k2tog] 4x; knit across heel stitches. 32 instep stitches, 64 total stitches.

Toe

Round 1: *K1, SSK, knit to last 3 instep stitches, k2tog, k1; repeat from * across heel stitches.
Round 2: Knit.

Repeat Rounds 1-2 an additional 9x. 24 stitches. Then, repeat Round 1 only an additional 2x. 16 stitches.

Cut yarn, leaving a 14-16" tail. Graft toe closed using Kitchener Stitch.

Finishing

Weave in any remaining ends, dampen socks and lay flat to block or use sock blockers.

Materials:

Approximately 400 yards of fingering-weight yarn. *Sample uses Black Bunny Superwash Merino Classic (100% merino wool) in 'Kathy's Cape'.*

US1 (2.25mm) needles or size needed to obtain gauge

Yarn needle

Gauge:

8 stitches/11 rounds per inch in stockinette stitch

Size:

Foot circumference = approximately 8"

Nami

Designer's Notes:

This delightful blue colorway is nearly semi-solid, but has enough contrast that it can be slightly tricky to work with. Feather and fan is always a great option when working with hand-dyed yarns. Since this colorway immediately brought to mind ocean waves, I decided to give this fun cabled variation on traditional feather and fan a whirl. The socks are named for the Japanese word for wave.

The cables add some structure and stability to these socks that feather and fan is sometimes lacking. I opted for a simple garter stitch cuff that emphasizes the natural wave of the stitch pattern. The simple short-row heel can easily be converted to a flap heel if you prefer.

This sock would look great in any semi-solid or low-to-medium contrast variegated yarn. Although, if you're having difficulty with a particularly energetic hand-dyed colorway, you could give this pattern a try... It might turn out to be just what you need!

Leg

Cast on 78 stitches and divide them over dpns or circular needles as follows:

- If using dpns, place 26 stitches on needles 1 and 3, and 13 stitches on needles 2 and 4.
- If using circular needle(s), place 39 stitches on each needle.

The first 39 stitches of the round are the instep stitches and the last 39 stitches are the heel stitches. Join stitches into round being careful not to twist.

Round 1: Purl.
Round 2: Knit.
Round 3: Purl.
Round 4: Knit.

Begin working *Leg Wave Pattern* as follows (or from chart on p. 117) across all stitches:

Note: When working cables across the beginning of round on Round 4, you should not be moving the beginning of round location. The same number of stitches should remain on each needle, just swap their locations so you can complete the cables.

Leg Wave Pattern

(over 78 stitches and 4 rounds)
Round 1: K2tog 2x, *[k1, YO] 4x, k1, k2tog 4x; repeat from * to last 9 stitches, [k1, YO] 4x, k1, k2tog 2x.
Round 2: K2, *p9, k4; repeat from * to last 11 stitches, p9, k2.
Round 3: K11, *C4B, k9; repeat from * to last 2 stitches, C4B taking 2 stitches from beginning of next round.
Round 4 (worked on remaining 76 stitches after C4B at end of Round 3): Knit.

Repeat Rounds 1-4 until leg measures approximately 6" from cast-on edge (or desired length to top of heel flap), ending with Round 3 of pattern.

Heel

Work across instep stitches in Round 4 of *Leg Wave Pattern*. The heel flap will be worked back-and-forth over the 39 heel stitches.

Shape Top of Heel

Row 1 (RS): K38, W&T.
Row 2 (WS): P37, W&T.
Row 3: Knit to stitch before wrapped stitch (do not knit any wrapped stitches), W&T.
Row 4: Purl to stitch before wrapped stitch (do not purl any wrapped stitches), W&T.
Repeat Rows 3-4 an additional 11x – there are now 13 wrapped stitches on either side of 13 unwrapped center stitches.

Shape Bottom of Heel

Row 1 (RS): Knit to first wrapped stitch (do not knit across any wrapped stitches), lift wrap RS, turn.
Row 2 (WS): Sl1, purl to first wrapped stitch (do not purl across any wrapped stitches), lift wrap WS, turn.
Row 3: Sl1, knit to next wrapped stitch (just past the stitch unwrapped on the previous RS row), lift wrap RS, turn.
Row 4: Sl1, purl to next wrapped stitch (just past the stitch unwrapped on the previous WS row), lift wrap WS, turn.
Repeat Rows 3-4 an additional 10x – a single wrapped stitch remains on either side of heel.

Next Row: Sl1, knit to last wrapped stitch, lift wrap RS but do not turn. You should be at the beginning of the instep stitches.
Next Round: Work across instep stitches in Round 1 of *Instep Wave Pattern* from instructions below (or from chart on p. 117); lift wrap RS, knit to end of heel stitches.

Instep Wave Pattern

(over 39 stitches and 4 rounds)
Round 1: SSK twice, *[k1, YO] 4x, k1, k2tog 4x; repeat from *, [k1, YO] 4x, k1, k2tog 2x.

Round 2: K2, *p9, k4; repeat from *, p9, k2.

Round 3: K11, C4B, k9, C4B, k11.

Round 4: Knit.

Next Round: Work across instep stitches in next round of *Instep Wave Pattern*; k2tog, knit to last 2 heel stitches, SSK.

Repeat last round once more. 74 stitches, 39 instep and 35 heel.

Foot

Continuing in the round, work *Instep Wave Pattern* across the 39 instep stitches and knit the 35 heel stitches until foot from start of heel turn to needles measures approximately 2" less than desired finished bottom-of-foot length, ending with Round 4 of pattern.

Toe

Round 1: SSK 2x, knit to last 4 instep stitches, k2tog 2x; knit to end of heel stitches. 70 stitches.

Round 2: Knit.

Round 3: *K1, SSK, knit to last 3 instep stitches, k2tog, k1; repeat from * across heel stitches. 66 stitches.

Repeat Rounds 2-3 an additional 9x. 30 stitches. Repeat Round 3 only an additional 3x. 18 stitches.

Cut yarn, leaving a 14-16" tail. Graft toe closed using Kitchener Stitch. Weave tail in on WS to secure.

Finishing

Weave in any remaining ends, dampen socks and lay flat to block or use sock blockers.

Leg Wave Pattern

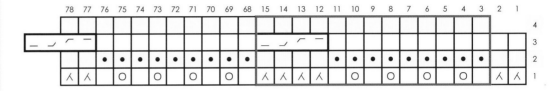

Instep Wave Pattern

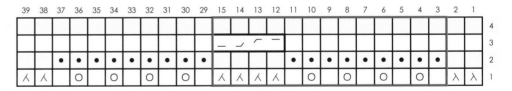

□	knit
•	purl
λ	SSK
⅄	k2tog
O	YO
▭	C4B
□	pattern repeat

Materials:

One Gradience sock set (four 100 yd skeins) or 200 yds each of two colors fingering-weight yarn. *Sample uses Unique Sheep Verve (100% superwash merino wool) in 'Fire Starter'.*

US1-1/2 (2.25mm) needles or size needed to obtain gauge

Yarn needle, stitch markers

Gauge:

8 stitches/10 rounds per inch in stockinette stitch

Size:

Foot circumference = approximately 7-1/2 (8-3/4)"
Note: This sock should be knit with very little negative ease due to the unstretchy nature of the colorwork.

Flamewalker

Designer's Notes:

The Unique Sheep's Gradience colorway series is a delight just to look at, much less knit with! Instead of just finding a stitch pattern that would work nicely with the gradience concept (which starts out with a different shade of semi-solid on each end with transition skeins in the middle), I wanted to figure out something that would really show it off in a way I hadn't seen before.

I chose a basic colorwork pattern and transitioned it in opposite directions. Starting with the two semi-solids together, the gradients then work in opposite directions so the top of the sock is like a photo-negative of the toe, with the pattern fading out of focus over the arch where the middle skeins of the gradient are worked together.

Of course, gradience yarn isn't required for this pattern - it will also look spectacular worked in two nicely contrasting solids, or in a solid paired with a contrasting variegated colorway. This colorwork concept is meant to be played with!

This was the October 2010 Indie Socks CSK featured pattern.

Toe

With Gradience #4 (or CC), using Judy's Magic Cast On or your favorite toe-up cast-on, cast on 30 (35) heel stitches and 30 (35) instep stitches or 60 (70) total stitches, dividing them over your selected needles.

The toe will be worked back and forth across the heel stitches.

Shape Bottom of Toe

Row 1 (RS): K29 (34), W&T.
Row 2 (WS): P28 (33), W&T.
Row 3: Knit to stitch before wrapped stitch (do not knit across any wrapped stitches), W&T.
Row 4: Purl to stitch before wrapped stitch (do not purl across any wrapped stitches), W&T.
Repeat Rows 3-4 an additional 8 (10) x - there are now 10 (12) wrapped stitches on either side of 10 (11) unwrapped center stitches.

Shape Top of Toe

Row 1 (RS): Knit to first wrapped stitch (do not knit across any wrapped stitches), lift wrap RS, turn.
Row 2 (WS): Purl to first wrapped stitch (do not purl across any wrapped stitches), lift wrap WS, turn.
Row 3: Sl1, knit to next wrapped stitch (just past the stitch unwrapped on the previous RS row), lift wrap RS, turn.

Row 4: Sl1, purl to next wrapped stitch (just past the stitch unwrapped on the previous WS row), lift wrap WS, turn.
Repeat Rows 3-4 an additional 7 (9)x - a single wrapped stitch remains on either side of toe.

Next Round: Sl1, k28 (33), lift wrap RS but do not turn; knit across heel stitches.
Next Round: Lift wrap RS to hide final wrap (which is at beginning of round), knit to end of round.

Foot

Begin working all stitches in color pattern from chart on p. 122. You will begin working using Gradience #1 as MC and Gradience #4 as CC (if using two colors instead of a Gradience set, join MC and work colors directly as charted).

If you are using the Gradience yarn, please be sure to look for and read all notes 'For Gradience Users Only' throughout the pattern before you start knitting each section.

For Gradience Users Only: When sock measures approximately 4" from tip of toe, join Gradience #3 and alternate it with Gradience #4 (as CC) every other round for 6 rounds. For example, if you are on Round 1 of the chart when you join Gradience #3, work Round 1 using Gradience #3 as CC, work Round 2 using Gradience #4 as CC, work Round 3 using Gradience #3 as CC, etc. Continue using Gradience #1 as MC. Once the 6 rounds have been worked, break Gradience #4 and use only Gradience #3 as CC.

Continue in color pattern until foot measures approximately 4-1/2" less than desired finished foot length.

Gusset

Round 1: Work Round 1 of Right Gusset Chart (on p. 122) over first 2 heel stitches, pm, work color pattern as established starting on stitch 3 (3) of chart and ending on stitch 8 (3) to last 2 heel stitches, pm, work Round 1 of Left Gusset Chart over last 2 heel stitches; work instep stitches in color pattern as established.
Round 2: Work next round of Right Gusset Chart to marker || work color pattern as established to next marker || work next round of Left Gusset Chart to end of heel stitches; work instep stitches in color pattern as established.
Repeat Round 2 until gusset charts are complete (Gradience users read note below first). 60 (65) heel stitches. Work to end of instep stitches in pattern. Break MC and remove markers.

For Gradience Users Only: When sock measures approximately 5-1/2" from tip of toe, join Gradience #2 and alternate it with Gradience #1 (as MC) every other round for 6 rounds. Continue using Gradience #3 as CC. Once the 6 rounds have been worked, break Gradience #1 and use only Gradience #2 as MC.

Turn Heel

Row 1 (RS): With CC, k44 (49), W&T.
Row 2 (WS): P28 (33), W&T.
Row 3: Knit to stitch before wrapped stitch (do not knit any wrapped stitches), W&T.
Row 4: Purl to stitch before wrapped stitch (do not purl any wrapped stitches), W&T.
Repeat Rows 3-4 an additional 8 (10)x – there are now 10 (12) wrapped stitches on either side of 10 (11) unwrapped center stitches.

Next Round: With RS facing, knit to end of heel stitches, lifting wraps RS as you encounter them. Rejoin MC at start of instep stitches and work across instep stitches in pattern as established.

Heel Flap

Drop MC at end of instep stitches but do not break. Work the heel flap back and forth with CC only.

Row 1 (RS): K44 (49) lifting remaining wraps RS as you encounter them, SSK, turn.
Row 2 (WS): [Sl1, p1] 14 (17)x, sl1 (0), p2tog, turn.
Row 3: Sl1, k28 (33), SSK, turn.
Row 4: Repeat Row 2.
Repeat Rows 3-4 an additional 13x. As you do this, you are slowly working up the edge of the gusset and forming the heel flap as you go. At the end, you are left with 60 (70) stitches, 30 (35) instep and 30 (35) heel.

Turn so RS is facing - you are at the start of the heel stitches. Pick up MC and resume working color pattern as established.

For Gradience Users Only: When you pick up MC to begin working leg, you will swap Gradience #2 and Gradience #3 so that Gradience #2 is now CC and Gradience #3 is now MC.

Leg

Work in color pattern as established until leg measures 4" or 1" less than desired finished length from top of heel flap.

For Gradience Users Only: When leg measures 1/4" from top of heel flap, join Gradience #4 and alternate it with Gradience #3 (as MC) every other round for 6 rounds. Continue using Gradience #2 as CC. Once the 6 rounds have been worked, break Gradience #3 and use only Gradience #4 as MC.

When leg measures 2" from top of heel flap, join Gradience #1 and alternate it with Gradience #2 (as CC) every other round for 6 rounds. Continue using Gradience #4 as MC. Once the 6 rounds have been worked, break Gradience #2 and use only Gradience #1 as CC.

Cuff

Loosely work 1" of k1, p1 rib using CC to knit and MC to purl. Break MC. Break CC leaving a 24-28" tail.

Thread CC tail onto yarn needle and bind off all stitches loosely using a sewn bind off as follows:

1. Thread yarn tail through first two stitches on the left needle as if to purl, leaving both stitches on the needle.

2. Thread the yarn tail through the right-most stitch on the left needle as if to knit, slipping it over to the right needle so that it's at the end of the round of stitches to be bound off.

3. Repeat Step 1.

4. Thread the yarn tail through the right-most stitch on the left needle as if to knit, slipping it off the needle in the process.

Repeat Steps 3 and 4 until one stitch remains (this is the stitch that was moved to the right needle in Step 2). Slip this stitch off the needle and fasten off.

Finishing

Weave in all ends, dampen socks and lay flat to block or use sock blockers.

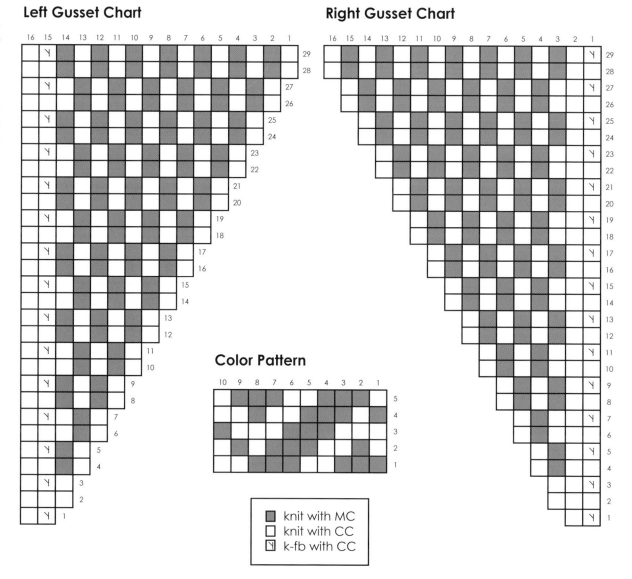

Left Gusset Chart

Right Gusset Chart

Color Pattern

knit with MC
knit with CC
k-fb with CC

Spicy Yarns

Abstract Fiber
Hand Dyed Yarn
Portland, Oregon

SuperSock

www.AbstractFiber.com

Materials:

Approximately 400 yards of fingering-weight yarn. *Sample uses Abstract Fiber SuperSock (100% superwash merino wool) in 'Portland'.*

US1 (2.25mm) needles or size needed to obtain gauge

Yarn needle

Gauge:

8-1/2 stitches/10 rounds per inch in stockinette stitch

Size:

Foot circumference = approximately 7-1/2"

Archery Socks

Designer's Notes:

This colorway gave me fits trying to find a stitch pattern that would work with it and not against it. Strong, deep colors are always challenging, and the first few designs I tried (including the lace motif that eventually ended up featured on the Tulip Socks) just didn't work.

After much thought, I decided to try something with simple, linear lace elements. Success! The stitch pattern I settled on after much swatching and deliberation allows the colors of the yarn to shine through without being muddied by an elaborate motif.

I opted for toe-up construction so that the little 'v's would be pointing like arrow tips down the length of the leg and foot. A gusset and heel flap add extra room across the instep. Lots of purled and twisted stitches help the brilliant little blips of color in this yarn really pop.

This was the September 2010 Indie Socks CSK featured pattern.

Toe

Using Judy's Magic Cast-On or your favorite toe-up cast on, cast on 7 instep stitches and 7 heel stitches (14 total stitches), dividing them over your selected needles.

Round 1: Knit.
Round 2: *K-fb, knit to last 2 instep stitches, k-fb, k1; repeat from * across heel stitches. 18 stitches.
Repeat Round 2 only an additional 3x. 30 stitches. Then, repeat Rounds 1-2 an additional 8x. 62 stitches, 31 instep and 31 heel. Knit one round even.

Foot

Begin working *Instep Pattern* Rounds 1-8 as follows (or from chart on p. 128) across the instep stitches. Continue working heel stitches in stockinette stitch.

Instep Pattern

(over 31 stitches and 8 rounds)
Round 1: YO, p2tog, p1, k2tog, YO, [k-tbl, YO, SSK, p1, p2tog, YO, p2, k2tog, YO] 2x, k-tbl, YO, SSK, p1, p2tog-tbl, YO.
Round 2: P3, k1, p1, [k-tbl, p1, k1, p5, k1, p1] 2x, k-tbl, p1, k1, p3.
Round 3: P2, k2tog, YO, p1, [k-tbl, p1, YO, SSK, p3, k2tog, YO, p1] 2x, k-tbl, p1, YO, SSK, p2.

Round 4: P2, k1, p2, [k-tbl, p2, k1, p3, k1, p2] 2x, k-tbl, p2, k1, p2.
Round 5: P1, k2tog, YO, p2, [k-tbl, p2, YO, SSK, p1, k2tog, YO, p2] 2x, k-tbl, p2, YO, SSK, p1.
Round 6: P1, k1, p3, [k-tbl, p3, k1, p1, k1, p3] 2x, k-tbl, p3, k1, p1.
Round 7: K2tog, YO, p3, [k-tbl, p3, YO, k3tog, YO, p3] 2x, k-tbl, p3, YO, SSK.
Round 8: K1, p4, [k-tbl, p4, k1, p4] 2x, k-tbl, p4, k1.
Repeat Rounds 1-8 until foot measures approximately 4-1/4" less than desired finished foot length.

Gusset

Round 1: Work instep stitches in *Instep Pattern* as established; k-fb in first heel stitch, knit to last 2 heel stitches, k-fb, k1.
Round 2: Work instep stitches in *Instep Pattern* as established; knit across all heel stitches.
Repeat Rounds 1-2 an additional 15x. 63 heel stitches.

Turn Heel

Work across instep stitches in pattern. The heel turn will be worked back-and-forth over the 63 heel stitches.
Row 1 (RS): K46, W&T.
Row 2 (WS): P29, W&T.
Row 3: Knit to stitch before wrapped stitch (do not knit any wrapped stitches), W&T.

Row 4: Purl to stitch before wrapped stitch (do not purl any wrapped stitches), W&T.
Repeat Rows 3-4 an additional 8x – there are now 10 wrapped stitches on either side of 11 unwrapped center stitches. Knit to end of heel stitches, lifting wraps RS as they are encountered, then work across instep stitches in pattern.

Heel Flap

Work the heel flap back and forth.
Row 1 (RS): K16, then k30 lifting remaining wraps RS as you encounter them, SSK, turn.
Row 2 (WS): [Sl1, p1] 15x, p2tog, turn.
Row 3: Sl1, k29, SSK, turn.
Row 4: Repeat Row 2.
Repeat Rows 3-4 an additional 13x, then work Row 3 once more but do not turn. As you do this, you are slowly working up the edge of the gusset and forming the heel flap as you go. At the end, you are left with 63 stitches, 31 instep and 32 heel.

Next Round: Work across instep stitches in pattern; k2tog, knit to end of heel stitches. 62 stitches, 31 instep and 31 heel.

Leg

Continue to work the instep stitches in pattern as established. Begin working the heel stitches in *Back Leg Pattern* Rounds 1-8 as follows (or from chart on p. 128) across all stitches. Begin the pattern on the same round as the instep pattern so that the design will line up on both sides of the leg.

Back Leg Pattern

(over 31 stitches and 8 rounds)

Round 1: K-tbl, p2, k2tog, YO, [k-tbl, YO, SSK, p1, p2tog, YO, p2, k2tog, YO] 2x, k-tbl, YO, SSK, p2, k-tbl.

Round 2: K-tbl, p2, k1, p1, [k-tbl, p1, k1, p5, k1, p1] 2x, k-tbl, p1, k1, p2, k-tbl.

Round 3: K-tbl, p1, k2tog, YO, p1, [k-tbl, p1, YO, SSK, p3, k2tog, YO, p1] 2x, k-tbl, p1, YO, SSK, p1, k-tbl.

Round 4: K-tbl, p1, k1, p2, [k-tbl, p2, k1, p3, k1, p2] 2x, k-tbl, p2, k1, p1, k-tbl.

Round 5: K-tbl, k2tog, YO, p2, [k-tbl, p2, YO, SSK, p1, k2tog, YO, p2] 2x, k-tbl, p2, YO, SSK, k-tbl.

Round 6: K-tbl, k1, p3, [k-tbl, p3, k1, p1, k1, p3] 2x, k-tbl, p3, k1, k-tbl.

Round 7: K2tog, YO, p3, [k-tbl, p3, YO, k3tog, YO, p3] 2x, k-tbl, p3, YO, SSK.

Round 8: K-tbl, p4, [k-tbl, p4, k1, p4] 2x, k-tbl, p4, k-tbl.

Work in pattern until the leg measures approximately 5" from top of heel flap (or 1/2" less than desired finished length), ending with Round 8 of patterns.

Cuff

Work cuff in ribbing pattern as follows:

Round 1: *[K-tbl, p1, k2, p1] 6x, k-tbl; repeat from * across heel stitches.

Repeat Round 1 an additional 7x.

Bind off all stitches loosely as follows: K1, *YO, k1, using tip of left needle, pass 2nd and 3rd stitches on right needle over 1st stitch on right needle (one stitch remains on right needle); repeat from * until all stitches are bound off. Fasten off.

Finishing

Weave in any remaining ends, dampen socks and lay flat to block or use sock blockers.

Instep Pattern

31	30	29	28	27	26	25	24	23	22	21	20	19	18	17	16	15	14	13	12	11	10	9	8	7	6	5	4	3	2	1	
B	•			•	B	•			•	B	•			•	B	•			•	B	•			•	B	•			•	B	Rib Round 1

31	30	29	28	27	26	25	24	23	22	21	20	19	18	17	16	15	14	13	12	11	10	9	8	7	6	5	4	3	2	1	
	•	•	•	B	•	•	•	•	•		•	•	•	B	•	•	•	•		•	•	•	B	•	•	•	•	•			8
λ	O	•	•	B	•	•	•	O	⋏	O	•	•	•	B	•	•	•	O	⋏	O	•	•	B	•	•	•	O	λ			7
•		•	•	B	•	•	•		•		•	•	•	B	•	•	•		•		•	•	B	•	•	•	•				6
•	λ	O	•	B	•	•	O	⋏	•	λ	O	•	•	B	•	•	O	⋏	•	λ	O	•	B	•	•	O	λ				5
•			•	B	•	•		•	•	•		•	•	B	•	•		•	•		•	•	B	•	•						4
•	•	λ	O	B	•	O	⋏	•	•	•	λ	O	•	B	•	O	⋏	•	•	•	λ	O	B	•	O	λ					3
•	•	•	•	B	•	•	•	•	•	•	•	•	•	B	•	•	•	•	•	•	•	•	B	•	•	•	•				2
O	△	•	λ	O	B	O	⋏	•	•	O	△	•	λ	O	B	O	⋏	•	•	O	△	•	λ	O	B	O	⋏	•	△	O	1

Back Leg Pattern

31	30	29	28	27	26	25	24	23	22	21	20	19	18	17	16	15	14	13	12	11	10	9	8	7	6	5	4	3	2	1	
B	•			•	B	•			•	B	•			•	B	•			•	B	•			•	B	•			•	B	Rib Round 1

31	30	29	28	27	26	25	24	23	22	21	20	19	18	17	16	15	14	13	12	11	10	9	8	7	6	5	4	3	2	1	
B	•	•	•	B	•	•	•		•		•	•	•	B	•	•	•		•	•	•	•	B	•	•	•	•	B		B	8
λ	O	•	•	B	•	•	•	O	⋏	O	•	•	•	B	•	•	•	O	⋏	O	•	•	B	•	•	•	O	λ		⋏	7
B		•	•	B	•	•	•		•		•	•	•	B	•	•	•		•	•	•	•	B	•	•	•		B		B	6
B	λ	O	•	B	•	•	O	⋏	•	λ	O	•	•	B	•	•	O	⋏	•	λ	O	•	B	•	•	O	λ	B		B	5
B	•			•	B	•		•	•	•		•	•	B	•	•		•	•		•	•	B	•	•			B		B	4
B	•	λ	O	•	B	•	O	⋏	•	•	•	λ	O	•	B	•	O	⋏	•	•	λ	O	•	B	•	O	λ	•	B	B	3
B	•	•		•	B	•	•	•	•	•	•	•	•		B	•	•	•	•	•	•	•		B	•	•		•	B	B	2
B	•	•	λ	O	B	O	⋏	•	•	O	△	•	λ	O	B	O	⋏	•	•	O	△	•	λ	O	B	O	⋏	•	•	B	1

Legend:

Symbol	Meaning
□	knit
B	k-tbl
•	purl
O	YO
λ	SSK
⋏	k2tog
⋏	k3tog
△	p2tog
△	p2tog-tbl
⋀	S2KP

There is a tendency for sock designs to come in a single size (women's M) or a very limited range of common sizes. What happens if your feet fall outside this range?

For a simply-patterned sock, you have a couple different options. You can add extra stitches (add the same number to both the instep and the heel for the easiest math) and recalculate your toe and heel. There are a number of sock calculators available on the internet that can assist you with this if you don't feel comfortable doing it yourself. These extra stitches can then be worked in rib or simply knitted, depending on how you think they will look with the rest of the design.

If you're willing to do a bit more math, it's possible to add a half or whole repeat of a stitch pattern depending on how many stitches are in the pattern and how much width you need to add to the sock. Drawing out the pattern on a piece of graph paper or in an Excel spreadsheet and then playing around with the placement of the extra stitches can help with this process (or confirm that this is a sock better resized by other methods).

If you'd rather not redo the math or the sock has an extremely complex stitch pattern, you can still resize the sock to fit by working on larger or smaller needles to change the circumference of the sock.

You will need to consider switching the weight of yarn you're using for the sock so that your gauge doesn't get too loose and result in a flimsy fabric. This method works best if you haven't already set your heart on a specific yarn for this particular pattern.

You can change your sock circumference quite a bit by tweaking the gauge by a stitch or two. For example, a 64 stitch sock will have a circumference of about 8" with a gauge of eight stitches per inch. If you switch yarn and needles for a seven stitch-per-inch gauge, the sock ends up with a circumference of 9". Switching to yarn and needles for a six stitch-per-inch gauge results in a 10-1/2" sock.

I highly recommend using sport-weight or dk-weight yarn at a seven stitch-per-inch gauge and worsted-weight yarn at a six stitch-per-inch gauge. You'll end up with a thicker sock than you would if using fingering-weight yarn, but it will be durable, fit your foot, and won't require any complicated math.

Tips & Tricks: Resizing

SOCKS THAT ROCK®
100% SUPERWASH MERINO - MEDIUMWEIGHT
HAND DYED FIBER
approx: 380 yds / 347m, 5.5 oz / 155g

colorway: Scum Bubbles

BLUE
MOON
Fiber Arts®

Materials:

Approximately 380 yards of heavy fingering or sport-weight yarn. *Sample uses Blue Moon Fiber Arts Socks That Rock Mediumweight (100% superwash merino) in 'Scum Bubbles'.*

US2 (2.75mm) needles or size needed to obtain gauge

Yarn needle, cable needle

Gauge:

7-1/2 stitches/10 rounds per inch in stockinette stitch

Size:

Foot circumference = approximately 7-1/2" (this stitch pattern is quite stretchy)

Pachinko

Designer's Notes:

This engaging colorway is a deceptive one. While the colors are relatively close in value, and it doesn't look like it should cause trouble with a wide range of patterns, I found it to be a bit pickier than I'd anticipated.

Because of the twist of the yarn and the muted colors, I found that cables virtually disappeared. My first attempt at swatching this yarn was with the cable and lace pattern I ultimately used for the Muir Woods socks with great success. I wasn't loving it, so I decided to move away from cables and toward this graphic lace pattern.

I swatched a bit, and was moderately happy with the results. It was only when I actually put the sock on my foot that the magic happened. I absolutely adore the results when the lace opens up and the stacked decreases expand into their very pronounced zigzag pattern. In this case, not only did I have to swatch, I had to actually wear the socks to determine I'd found the right stitch/colorway mix!

Leg

Cast on 60 stitches and divide them over dpns or circular needles as follows:

- If using dpns, place 19 stitches on Needle 1, 14 stitches on Needle 2, 16 stitches on Needle 3 and 11 stitches on Needle 4
- If using circular needle(s), place 33 stitches on Needle 1 and 27 stitches on Needle 2.

The first 33 stitches of the round are the instep stitches and the last 27 stitches are the heel stitches. Join stitches into round being careful not to twist.

Work in k1, p1 rib for 8 rounds.

Begin working *Ribbon Lace Pattern* as follows (or from chart) across all stitches:

Ribbon Lace Pattern

(over a multiple of 10 stitches and 12 rounds)

Round 1: *SSK, YO, k5, k2tog, YO, k1; repeat from * to end of round.

Round 2: K1, *YO, k2tog, k3, k2tog, k1, YO, k2; repeat from * to last 9 stitches, YO, k2tog, k3, k2tog, k1, YO, k1.

Round 3: *SSK, YO, k3, k2tog, k2, YO, k1; repeat from * to end of round.

Round 4: K1, *YO, k2tog, k1, k2tog, k3, YO, k2; repeat from * to last 9 stitches, YO, k2tog, k1, k2tog, k3, YO, k1.

Round 5: *SSK, YO, k2, SSK, k3, YO, k1; repeat from * to end of round.

Round 6: K1, *YO, k2tog, k1, SSK, k3, YO, k2; repeat from * to last 9 stitches, YO, k2tog, k1, SSK, k3, YO, k1.

Round 7: *SSK, YO, k2, YO, SSK, k4; repeat from * to end of round.

Round 8: K1, *YO, k2tog, k1, YO, k1, SSK, k4; repeat from * to last 9 stitches, YO, k2tog, k1, YO, k1, SSK, k3.

Round 9: *SSK, YO, k2, YO, k2, SSK, k2; repeat from * to end of round.

Round 10: K1, *YO, k2tog, k1, YO, k3, SSK, k2; repeat from * to last 9 stitches, YO, k2tog, k1, YO, k3, SSK, k1.

Round 11: *SSK, YO, k2, YO, k3, k2tog, k1; repeat from * to end of round.

Round 12: K1, *YO, k2tog, k1, YO, k3, k2tog, k2; repeat from * to last 9 stitches, YO, k2tog, k1, YO, k3, k2tog, k1.

Repeat Rounds 1-12 until leg measures approximately 5" from start (or desired length to top of heel flap).

Heel Flap

Work across instep stitches in pattern as established. The heel flap will then be worked back-and-forth over the 27 heel stitches.

Row 1 (RS): [Sl1, k1] 13x, k1, turn.
Row 2: Sl1, purl to end of row, turn.

Ribbon Lace Pattern

10	9	8	7	6	5	4	3	2	1	
	∧				O		∧	O		12
	∧				O			O	λ	11
	λ				O		∧	O		10
		λ			O			O	λ	9
			λ		O		∧	O		8
				λ	O			O	λ	7
	O				λ		∧	O		6
	O				λ			O	λ	5
	O				∧		∧	O		4
	O			∧				O	λ	3
	O		∧				∧	O		2
	O	∧						O	λ	1

□	knit
O	YO
λ	SSK
∧	k2tog

Repeat Rows 1-2 an additional 13x.

Turn Heel

Row 1 (RS): Sl1, k13, SSK, k1, turn.
Row 2: Sl1, p2, p2tog, p1, turn.
Row 3: Sl1, knit to stitch before gap formed by previous row's turn, SSK, k1, turn.
Row 4: Sl1, purl to stitch before gap formed by previous row's turn, p2tog, p1, turn.
Repeat Rows 3-4 until all heel flap

stitches have been worked. 15 heel stitches remain.

Shape Gusset

Knit across the 15 heel stitches. Working up the side of the heel flap with the same needle, pu 14 stitches. Work instep stitches in pattern as established. Working down the other side of the heel flap with an empty dpn or empty end of second circular needle, pu 14 stitches. 43 heel stitches.

If using dpns, knit the first 8 stitches from the second heel needle onto the first so there are approximately an equal number of heel stitches on each needle.

To get back to the beginning of the round, knit to the last 3 heel stitches, k2tog, k1. 42 heel stitches.
Round 1: Work instep stitches in pattern as established; k1, SSK, knit to end of heel stitches.
Round 2: Work instep stitches in pattern as established; knit to last 3 heel stitches, k2tog, k1.
Repeat Rounds 1-2 an additional 7x. 26 heel stitches, 59 total stitches.

Foot

Continue to work instep stitches in pattern as established and heel stitches in stockinette stitch until foot

from start of heel turn to needles measures approximately 2" less than desired finished bottom-of-foot length.

Next Round: Work instep stitches in pattern, omitting all YOs; knit to end of heel stitches. 26 instep stitches, 52 total stitches.

Toe

Round 1: *K1, SSK, knit to last 3 instep stitches, k2tog, k1; repeat from * across heel stitches.
Round 2: Knit.

Repeat Rounds 1-2 an additional 7x. 20 stitches. Then, repeat Round 1 only an additional 2x. 12 stitches.

Cut yarn, leaving a 14-16" tail. Graft toe closed using Kitchener Stitch.

Finishing

Weave in any remaining ends, dampen socks and lay flat to block or use sock blockers.

CraftsMeow

www.CraftsMeow.etsy.com

Hand-dyed yarn
Fast shipping
Unique stitch markers

Materials:

Approximately 400 yards of fingering-weight yarn. *Sample uses CraftsMeow Soft Serve (100% superwash merino) in 'Witch's Brew'.*

US1 (2.25mm) needles or size needed to obtain gauge

Yarn needle

Gauge:

8-1/2 stitches/12 rounds per inch in stockinette stitch

Size:

Foot circumference = approximately 7-1/2" (this pattern is quite stretchy)

memento mori

Designer's Notes:

With a yarn as dark as Witch's Brew, finding a pattern that isn't totally hidden by the colorway is a real challenge. In this case, I took the Jack-in-the-Pulpit motif from Barbara Walker's *A Second Treasury of Knitting Patterns* and modified it to be worked in the round.

When worked in top-down socks, it reminds me of tiny skulls, little ghosts, or possibly Darth Vader's mask. *Memento Mori* artwork often features skulls or other themes of death, serving to remind humankind of their mortality.

The stitch pattern is a little fiddly at first, but keep at it until you get the hang of it. You will find that it has a nice rhythm and knits up like the wind. Regardless, it works nicely with this dark, high contrast colorway.

A linen stitch heel flap continues to break up the colors and adds interest to the back view. Start your Halloween (or Day of the Dead) socks today!

This was the July 2011 Indie Socks CSA featured pattern.

Leg

Cast on 72 stitches and divide them over dpns or circular needles as follows:

- If using dpns, place 18 stitches on each needle.
- If using circular needle(s), place 36 stitches on each needle.

The first 36 stitches of the round are the instep stitches and the last 36 stitches are the heel stitches. Join stitches into round being careful not to twist.

Round 1: *K1, p1, k1; repeat from * to end of round.

Repeat Round 1 an additional 7x.

Begin working *Skull Pattern* as follows across all stitches.

Skull Pattern

(over a multiple of 7-11 stitches and 8 rounds)

Round 1: *K1, p1, k2tog, p1, SSK, p1, k1; repeat from * to end of round. 56 stitches, 28 instep and 28 heel.

Round 2: *K1, p5, k1; repeat from * to end of round.

Round 3: *K1, p3, YO, p2, k1; repeat from * to end of round. 64 stitches, 32 instep and 32 heel.

Round 4: *K1, p2, sl1 wyif, drop YO off left needle, YO (take yarn to back over top of needle, crossing over sl1 in process), p2, k1; repeat from * to end of round.

Round 5: *K1, p2, sl2 wyif (you are slipping the sl1 from the previous round plus the YO crossing over it), YO (take yarn to back over top of needle, crossing over sl1 and slipped YO in process), p2, k1; repeat from * to end of round. 72 stitches 36 instep and 36 heel.

Round 6: *K1, p2, sl3 wyif (you are slipping the sl1 from Round 2 and the 2 YOs crossing over it), YO (take yarn to back over top of needle, crossing over sl1 and 2 slipped YOs in process), p2, k1; repeat from * to end of round. 80 stitches, 40 instep and 40 heel.

Round 7: *K1, p2, sl4 wyif (you are slipping the sl1 from Round 2 and the 3 YOs crossing over it), YO (take yarn to back over top of needle, crossing over sl1 and 3 slipped YOs in process), p2, k1; repeat from * to end of round. 88 stitches, 44 instep and 44 heel.

Round 8: *K1, p2, knit the 4 crossed over YOs together (being careful not to knit the sl1 from Round 2 in with them) leaving them on the left-hand needle, purl the sl1 from Round 2 (you will have to reach behind and possibly pull the sl1 out from under the crossed over YOs - be sure to insert the needle from the back, behind the clump of YOs, and do not purl the YOs in with the sl1), knit the 4 crossed YOs together again and slip them off the left-hand needle, p2, k1; repeat from * to end of round. 72 stitches, 36 instep and 36 heel.

Repeat Rounds 1-8 until cuff measures approximately 5-1/2" from cast-on edge or desired finished length to top of heel flap, ending with Round 2 of pattern.

Heel Flap

Work across instep stitches in Round 3 of pattern. The heel flap will now be worked back-and-forth over the 28 heel stitches.

Row 1 (RS): Sl1, [k1, sl1-wyif] 13x, k1, turn.
Row 2: Sl1, purl to end of row, turn.
Row 3: Sl1, [sl1-wyif, k1] 13x, k1, turn.
Row 4: Sl1, purl to end of row, turn.

Repeat Rows 1-4 an additional 7x.

Turn Heel

Row 1 (RS): Sl1, k14, SSK, k1, turn.
Row 2: Sl1, p3, p2tog, p1, turn.
Row 3: Sl1, knit to stitch before gap formed by previous row's turn, SSK, k1, turn.
Row 4: Sl1, purl to stitch before gap formed by previous row's turn, p2tog, p1, turn.

Repeat Rows 3-4 until all heel flap stitches have been worked. 16 heel stitches remain.

Shape Gusset

Knit across the 16 heel stitches. Working up the side of the heel flap with the same needle, pu 16 stitches. Work instep stitches in Round 4 of pattern. Working down the other side of the heel flap with an empty dpn or empty end of second circular needle, pu 16 stitches. 48 heel stitches.

If using dpns, knit the first 8 stitches from the second heel needle onto the first so there are an equal number of heel stitches on each needle.

To get back to the beginning of the round, knit to the end of the heel stitches.

Round 1: Work instep stitches in next round of instep pattern; knit to last 3 heel stitches, k2tog, k1.

Round 2: Work instep stitches in next round of instep pattern; k1, SSK, knit to end of heel stitches.

Repeat Rounds 1-2 an additional 9x. 28 heel stitches.

Foot

Continue to work instep stitches in pattern as established and heel stitches in stockinette stitch until foot from start of heel turn to needles measures approximately 1-1/2" less than desired finished bottom-of-foot length, ending with Round 2 of pattern.

Toe

Round 1: Knit.

Round 2: *K1, SSK, knit to last 3 instep stitches, k2tog, k1; repeat from * across heel stitches.

Repeat Rounds 1-2 an additional 9x. 16 stitches.

Cut yarn, leaving a 14-16" tail. Graft toe closed using Kitchener Stitch.

Finishing

Weave in any remaining ends, dampen socks and lay flat to block or use sock blockers.

Knitted Wit
fine treasures from a sassy girl

Materials:

Approximately 400 yards of fingering-weight yarn. *Sample uses Knitted Wit Superwash Merino Fingering Yarn (100% superwash merino) in 'Ladies That Lunch'.*

US1 (2.25mm) needles or size needed to obtain gauge

Yarn needle, cable needle

Gauge:

8 stitches/12 rounds per inch in stockinette stitch
11 stitches/13 rounds per inch in slip stitch pattern

Size:

Foot circumference = approximately 7-1/2 (8-1/2)"

Supernova

Designer's Notes:

What's to be done with that tempestuous variegated yarn that you just can't resist but that scoffs at any and all attempts to knit anything patterned with it? That was the question I struggled with as I started to work with this yarn.

I instantly felt a connection with this colorway (it reminds me of those Brach's Neapolitan candies I couldn't get enough of as a kid), and really looked forward to designing this sock. However, the contrast of light cream and dark brown, with light pink and darker rose in between, immediately asserted itself when I began to swatch.

Slipped stitch patterns are almost always the way to go when beating a feisty colorway like this into some semblance of submission. Purl stitches also add some interest and break up the colors differently than knits, so a slipped stitch design with a purl background ended up being ideal for this yarn.

This was the January 2011 Indie Socks CSK featured pattern.

Leg

Cast on 70 (78) stitches and divide them over dpns or circular needles as follows:

- If using dpns, place 18 (20) stitches on needles 1 and 3, and 17 (19) stitches on needles 2 and 4
- If using circular needle(s), place 35 (39) stitches on each needle.

The first 35 (39) stitches of the round are the instep stitches and the last 35 (39) stitches are the heel stitches. Join stitches into round being careful not to twist.

Round 1: *P1 (2), [k1, p2] 2x, k1, p1, k1, p1 (2), [k1, p1] 6x, k1, p1 (2), k1, p1, [k1, p2] 2x, k1, p1 (2); repeat from * across heel stitches.
Repeat Round 1 an additional 5x.

Begin working *Slip Panel Pattern* as follows (or from chart on p. 142 or 143) across all stitches:

Slip Panel Pattern

(over a multiple of 35 (39) stitches and 18 rounds)
Round 1: P1 (2), [sl1, k2] 3x, p1 (2), k1, sl1, k9, sl1, k1, p1 (2), [k2, sl1] 3x, p1 (2).
Round 2: P1 (2), [C2F, k1] 3x, p2 (3), T2F, p3, k1, p3, T2B, p2 (3), [k1, C2B] 3x, p1 (2).

Round 3: P1 (2), k1, [sl1, k2] 2x, sl1, k1, p3 (4), sl1, p3, k1, p3, sl1, p3 (4), k1, [sl1, k2] 2x, sl1, k1, p1 (2).
Round 4: P1 (2), [k1, C2F] 3x, p3 (4), T2F, p2, k1, p2, T2B, p3 (4), [C2B, k1] 3x, p1 (2).
Round 5: P1 (2), [k2, sl1] 2x, k3, p4 (5), sl1, p2, k1, p2, sl1, p4 (5), k3, [sl1, k2] 2x, p1 (2).
Round 6: P1 (2), k2, C2F, k1, C2F, k2, p4 (5), T2F, p1, k1, p1, T2B, p4 (5), k2, C2B, k1, C2B, k2, p1 (2).
Round 7: P1 (2), [sl1, k2] 3x, p5 (6), sl1, p1, k1, p1, sl1, p5 (6), [k2, sl1] 3x, p1 (2).
Round 8: P1 (2), [C2F, k1] 3x, p1 (2), k4, C2F, k1, C2B, k4, p1 (2), [k1, C2B] 3x, p1 (2).
Round 9: P1 (2), k1, [sl1, k2] 2x, sl1, k1, p15 (17), k1, [sl1, k2] 2x, sl1, k1, p1 (2).
Round 10: P1 (2), [k1, C2F] 3x, p1 (2), k5, sl1, k1, sl1, k5, p1 (2), [C2B, k1] 3x, p1 (2).
Round 11: P1 (2), [k2, sl1] 2x, k3, p5 (6), T2B, k1, T2F, p5 (6), k3, [sl1, k2] 2x, p1 (2).
Round 12: P1 (2), k2, C2F, k1, C2F, k2, p5 (6), sl1, p1, k1, p1, sl1, p5 (6), k2, C2B, k1, C2B, k2, p1 (2).
Round 13: P1 (2), [sl1, k2] 3x, p4 (5), T2B, p1, k1, p1, T2F, p4 (5), [k2, sl1] 3x, p1 (2).
Round 14: P1 (2), [C2F, k1] 3x, p4 (5), sl1, p2, k1, p2, sl1, p4 (5), [k1, C2B] 3x, p1 (2).

Round 15: P1 (2), k1, [sl1, k2] 2x, sl1, k1, p3 (4), T2B, p2, k1, p2, T2F, p3 (4), k1, [sl1, k2] 2x, sl1, k1, p1 (2).
Round 16: P1 (2), [k1, C2F] 3x, p3 (4), sl1, p3, k1, p3, sl1, p3 (4), [C2B, k1] 3x, p1 (2).
Round 17: P1 (2), [k2, sl1] 2x, k3, p1 (2), k1, C2B, k7, C2F, k1, p1 (2), k3, [sl1, k2] 2x, p1 (2).
Round 18: P1 (2), k2, C2F, k1, C2F, k2, p15 (17), k2, C2B, k1, C2B, k2, p1 (2).

Repeat Rounds 1-18 until leg measures approximately 5" from start (or desired length to top of heel flap), ending with Round 18 of pattern.

Heel Flap

Work across instep stitches in pattern. The heel flap will then be worked back-and-forth over the 35 (39) heel stitches.

Row 1 (RS): [Sl1, k1] 17 (19)x, k1, turn.
Row 2: Sl1, purl to end of row, turn.
Repeat Rows 1-2 an additional 13 (15)x.

Turn Heel

Row 1 (RS): Sl1, k19 (22), SSK, k1, turn.
Row 2: Sl1, p6, p2tog, p1, turn.
Row 3: Sl1, knit to stitch before gap formed by previous row's turn, SSK, k1, turn.

Row 4: Sl1, purl to stitch before gap formed by previous row's turn, p2tog, p1, turn.
Repeat Rows 3-4 until all heel flap stitches have been worked. 21 (23) heel stitches remain.

Shape Gusset

Knit across the 21 (23) heel stitches. Working up the side of the heel flap with the same needle, pu 14 (16) stitches. Work instep stitches in pattern as established. Working down the other side of the heel flap with an empty dpn or empty end of second circular needle, pu 14 (16) stitches. 49 (55) heel stitches.

If using dpns, knit the first 11 (12) stitches from the second heel needle onto the first so there are an equal number of heel stitches on each needle.

To get back to the beginning of the round, knit to the last 3 heel stitches, k2tog, k1. 48 (54) heel stitches.

Round 1: Work instep stitches in pattern as established; k1, SSK, knit to end of heel stitches.
Round 2: Work instep stitches in pattern as established; knit to last 3 heel stitches, k2tog, k1.
Repeat Rounds 1-2 an additional 5 (6)x, then work Round 1 once more.

35 (39) heel stitches, 70 (78) total stitches.

Foot

Continue to work instep stitches in pattern as established and heel stitches in stockinette stitch until foot from start of heel turn to needles measures approximately 2 (2-1/4)" less than desired finished bottom-of-foot length, ending with Round 18 of pattern.

Toe

Round 1: *K1, SSK, knit to last 3 instep stitches, k2tog, k1; repeat from * across heel stitches.
Round 2: Knit.

Repeat Rounds 1-2 an additional 10 (12)x. 26 stitches. Then, repeat Round 1 only an additional 2x. 18 stitches.

Cut yarn, leaving a 14-16" tail. Graft toe closed using Kitchener Stitch.

Finishing

Weave in any remaining ends, dampen socks and lay flat to block or use sock blockers.

Slip Panel Pattern (7-1/2" size)

35 34 33 32 31 30 29 28 27 26 25 24 23 22 21 20 19 18 17 16 15 14 13 12 11 10 9 8 7 6 5 4 3 2 1

18 17 16 15 14 13 12 11 10 9 8 7 6 5 4 3 2 1

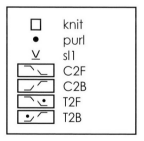

□	knit
•	purl
V	sl1
	C2F
	C2B
	T2F
	T2B

Slip Panel Pattern (8-1/2" size)

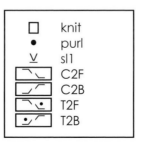

CEPHALOPOD
Yarns

Bugga!

...d- dyed, sport weight

...perwash merino

...mere / 10% Nylon

...2 yards

... US #2

Materials:

Approximately 400 yards of fingering-weight yarn. *Sample uses Cephalopod Yarns Bugga (70% superwash merino wool, 20% cashmere, 10% nylon) in 'Question Mark Butterfly'.*

US1 (2.25mm) needles or size needed to obtain gauge

Yarn needle

Gauge:

8 stitches/11 rounds per inch in stockinette stitch

Size:

Foot circumference = approximately 8"

Seesaw

Designer's Notes:

Dark colorways like this one, while easy on the eyes, are always a challenge to work with. Patterns tend to vanish into them, so I recommend steering clear of complex cables or other designs that require the stitches to stand out to look their best (although you never really know until you swatch).

Lace motifs can be a great option for darker yarns because they allow the skin to show through, creating visual interest and setting off the stitch pattern. The key is to find a lace design where the eyelets are the key element, as opposed to the decrease ribs. I found this zigzag pattern and swatched it up, hoping that the eyelets would steal the show. Luckily, they did!

This stitch pattern can grow quite a bit due to the large number of eyelets. If you find the leg too baggy, go down a needle size after the ribbing, and switch back to the larger needles for the heel and foot.

Leg

Cast on 62 stitches and divide them over dpns or circular needles as follows:

- If using dpns, place 16 stitches on each of needles 1 and 3, and 15 stitches on each of needles 2 and 4.
- If using circular needle(s), place 31 stitches on each needle.

The first 31 stitches of the round are the instep stitches and the last 31 stitches are the heel stitches. Join stitches into round being careful not to twist.

Round 1: *K2, [p1, k1] 13x, p1, k2; repeat from *.
Repeat Round 1 an additional 7x.

Begin working *Zigzag Pattern* as follows (or from chart on p. 148) across all stitches:

Zigzag Pattern

(over a multiple of 31 stitches and 22 rounds)

Round 1: *K2, [YO, SSK] 14x, k1; repeat from *.
Round 2 (and all even-numbered rounds): Knit.
Round 3: *K5, [YO, SSK] 5x, k2, [YO, SSK] 5x, k4; repeat from *.
Round 5: *K6, [YO, SSK] 4x, k4, [YO, SSK] 4x, k5; repeat from *.
Round 7: *K3, YO, SSK, k2, [YO, SSK] 3x, k2, YO, SSK, k2, [YO, SSK] 3x, k2, YO, SSK, k2; repeat from *.

Round 9: *K4, YO, SSK, k2, [YO, SSK] 2x, k1, k2tog, YO, k1, YO, SSK, k2, [YO, SSK] 2x, k1, k2tog, YO, k4; repeat from *.
Round 11: *K5, YO, SSK, k2, YO, SSK, k1, k2tog, YO, k3, YO, SSK, k2, YO, SSK, k1, k2tog, YO, k5; repeat from *.
Round 13: *K3, YO, SSK, k1, YO, SSK, k3, k2tog, YO, k2, YO, SSK, k1, YO, SSK, k3, k2tog, YO, k2, YO, SSK, k2; repeat from *.
Round 15: *K2, [YO, SSK] 2x, k1, YO, SSK, k1, k2tog, YO, k2, [YO, SSK] 2x, k1, YO, SSK, k1, k2tog, YO, k2, [YO, SSK] 2x, k1; repeat from *.
Round 17: *K3, [YO, SSK] 2x, k1, YO, SK2P, YO, k2, [YO, SSK] 3x, k1, YO, SK2P, YO, k2, [YO, SSK] 2x, k2; repeat from *.
Round 19: *K2, [YO, SSK] 3x, k1, YO, SSK, k1, [YO, SSK] 4x, k1, YO, SSK, k1, [YO, SSK] 3x, k1; repeat from *.
Round 21: *K3, [YO, SSK] 3x, k2, [YO, SSK] 5x, k2, [YO, SSK] 3x, k2; repeat from *.

Repeat Rounds 1-21 until leg measures approximately 5" from start (or desired length to top of heel flap).

Heel Flap

Work across instep stitches in pattern. The heel flap will now be worked back-and-forth over the 31 heel stitches.
Row 1 (RS): [Sl1, k1] 15x, k1, turn.

Row 2: Sl1, purl to end of row, turn.
Repeat Rows 1-2 an additional 13x.

Turn Heel

Row 1 (RS): Sl1, k16, SSK, k1, turn.
Row 2: Sl1, p2, p2tog, p1, turn.
Row 3: Sl1, knit to stitch before gap formed by previous row's turn, SSK, k1, turn.
Row 4: Sl1, purl to stitch before gap formed by previous row's turn, p2tog, p1, turn.
Repeat Rows 3-4 until all heel flap stitches have been worked. 17 heel stitches remain.

Shape Gusset

Knit across the 17 heel stitches. Working up the side of the heel flap with the same needle, pu 14 stitches. Work instep stitches in pattern as established. Working down the other side of the heel flap with an empty dpn or empty end of second circular needle, pu 14 stitches. 45 heel stitches.

If using dpns, knit the first 9 stitches from the second heel needle onto the first so there are approximately an equal number of heel stitches on each needle.

To get back to the beginning of the round, knit to the end of the heel stitches.

Round 1: Work instep stitches in pattern as established; knit to last 3 heel stitches, k2tog, k1.

Round 2: Work instep stitches in pattern as established; k1, SSK, knit to end of heel stitches.

Repeat Rounds 1-2 an additional 6x. 31 heel stitches, 62 total stitches.

Foot

Continue to work instep stitches in *Zigzag Pattern* as established and heel stitches in stockinette stitch until foot from start of heel turn to needles measures approximately 2" less than desired finished bottom-of-foot length.

Toe

Round 1: Knit.

Round 2: *K1, SSK, knit to last 3 instep stitches, k2tog, k1; repeat from * across heel stitches. 58 stitches.

Repeat Rounds 1-2 an additional 8x. 26 stitches. Then, repeat Round 1 only an additional 3x. 14 stitches.

Cut yarn, leaving a 14-16" tail. Graft toe closed using Kitchener Stitch.

Finishing

Weave in any remaining ends, dampen socks and lay flat to block or use sock blockers.

Zigzag Pattern

Legend:

Symbol	Meaning
□	knit
λ	SSK
⅄	k2tog
Λ	SK2P

31	30	29	28	27	26	25	24	23	22	21	20	19	18	17	16	15	14	13	12	11	10	9	8	7	6	5	4	3	2	1	
																															22
		λ	O	λ	O	λ	O			λ	O	λ	O	λ	O	λ	O	λ	O			λ	O	λ	O	λ	O				21
																															20
	λ	O	λ	O	λ	O		λ	O		λ	O	λ	O	λ	O	λ	O	λ	O		λ	O		λ	O	λ	O	λ	O	19
																															18
		λ	O	λ	O				O	Λ	O			λ	O	λ	O	λ	O			O	Λ	O			λ	O	λ	O	17
																															16
	λ	O	λ	O			O	⅄			λ	O		λ	O	λ	O		O	⅄		λ	O		λ	O	λ	O			15
																															14
		λ	O			O	⅄				λ	O		λ	O			O	⅄		λ	O		λ	O						13
																															12
				O	⅄		λ	O			λ	O			O	⅄		λ	O		λ	O									11
																															10
				O	⅄		λ	O	λ	O		λ	O		O	⅄		λ	O	λ	O		λ	O							9
																															8
	λ	O			λ	O	λ	O	λ	O			λ	O			λ	O	λ	O	λ	O			λ	O					7
																															6
				λ	O	λ	O	λ	O	λ	O					λ	O	λ	O	λ	O	λ	O								5
																															4
			λ	O	λ	O	λ	O	λ	O	λ	O			λ	O	λ	O	λ	O	λ	O	λ	O	λ	O					3
																															2
	λ	O	λ	O	λ	O	λ	O	λ	O	λ	O	λ	O	λ	O	λ	O	λ	O	λ	O	λ	O	λ	O	λ	O			1

I would like to say that our selection process was organized and rigorous, with specific criteria and lots of research, but...it was pretty much the opposite.

When I first came up with the idea for this book, I was so excited about it, I started asking every dyer within arm's reach if they'd like to be involved. I knew I wanted to include a few of the "big names" (e.g. Lorna's Laces, Blue Moon Fiber Arts, and Mountain Colors), but the selection process for the smaller dyers was completely undisciplined.

I started out with a bunch of folks whose yarns I'd worked with before, such as Abstract Fiber, Creatively Dyed, Shalimar Yarns, and Curious Creek. I added several friends to the mix (in Portland, it's hard to throw a skein of yarn without hitting a dyer in the face), and that brought in LavenderSheep, Knitted Wit, Pico(t) and Stitchjones. Finally, with Donna's help, I picked out several other dyers whom I'd met at various shows and/or knew were well-regarded by our circle of knitting friends.

While I did my best to choose dyers whose businesses are stable and who are in it for the long haul, it's possible that one or more of these folks will have sold or closed down their business by the time this book reaches your hands.

Dyeing yarn for a living is a hard job, even though it's lots of fun. People close up shop for all sorts of reasons. They may decide to go back to a full-time day job, their business may interfere with family obligations, or they just might not enjoy what they're doing any longer.

If you can't find a particular dyer whose yarn you'd like to use, don't despair. There are plenty of other options, and gaining confidence with yarn substitutions is a crucial skill for the serious knitter.

Ravelry is a great resource, and you can visit the Indie Socks Ravelry group at www.ravelry.com/groups/indie-socks-csk to ask questions about yarn substitutions and see what other knitters are using to make their projects.

It's great fun to scroll through the project pages and see everyone's socks – sometimes a particular sock may not strike your fancy as photographed in the book, but when you see it knit up in a different colorway, it could be just what you're looking for.

Our Dyer Selection Process

Blue Ridge Yarns

Footprints

Mossy Hollow

Superwash Merino Sock Yarn
300yds
2-3us need

Materials:

Approximately 300 yards of fingering-weight yarn in MC and 100 yards in CC. *Sample uses Blue Ridge Yarns Footprints (100% merino) in 'Mossy Hollow'.*

US1 (2.25mm) needles or size needed to obtain gauge
US2 (2.75mm) needles

Yarn needle, 2 cable needles

Gauge:

8 stitches/11 rounds per inch in stockinette stitch with smaller needles

Size:

Foot circumference = approximately 8"

Muir Woods

Designer's Notes:

You might be surprised to see cables used for this yarn, which has two of the hallmarks of cable disaster – darker colors and medium variegation. Imagine my surprise when, on a whim, I swatched this cable-and-lace diamond pattern and it turned out great!

It just goes to show, sometimes you can break the rules and end up with something fabulous. Don't be afraid to swatch!

This fun colorway, part of the Footprints series from Blue Ridge Yarns, comes with a small skein of matching solid-colored yarn. While it might be tempting to use the small skein for a colorwork motif, don't do it - it's dyed to match one of the shades in the variegated yarn. The color pattern will completely disappear anywhere the two greens line up next to each other. Better to use it for heels, toes and cuffs, like I did here.

Special Abbreviations and Techniques for this Pattern

TC6B: Sl2 to cable needle and hold in back, sl2 to second cable needle and hold in back but in front of first cable needle, k2, k2 from second cable needle, p2 from first cable needle.

TC6F: Sl2 to cable needle and hold in front, sl2 to second cable needle and hold in front but behind first cable needle, p2, k2 from second cable needle, k2 from first cable needle.

Note: When working TC6B and TC6F next to each other, keep stitches fairly tight to reduce laddering between the cables.

Toe

Using Judy's Magic Cast-On or your favorite toe-up cast on, smaller needles and CC, cast on 8 instep stitches and 8 heel stitches (16 total stitches), dividing them over your selected needles.

Round 1: Knit.
Round 2: *K-fb, knit to last 2 instep stitches, k-fb, k1; repeat from * across heel stitches. 20 stitches.
Repeat Round 2 twice more. 28 stitches. Then, repeat Rounds 1-2 an additional 8x. 60 stitches. Switch to MC

and work Rounds 1-2 twice more. 68 stitches. Switch back to CC and work Rounds 1-2 once more. 72 stitches. Break CC. With MC, knit one round even.

Foot

With MC only, begin working instep stitches in *Diamond Cables for Instep* as follows (or from chart on p. 156) and heel stitches in stockinette stitch. Work until foot measures 2" less than desired finished length from tip of toe.

Diamond Cables for Instep
(over 36 stitches and 32 rounds)
Round 1: YO, SSK, [k2tog, YO 2x, SSK] 2x, k2tog, YO, p2, k8, p2, YO, SSK, [k2tog, YO 2x, SSK] 2x, k2tog, YO.
Round 2: [K3, p1] 2x, k4, p2, k8, p2, [k3, p1] 2x, k4.
Round 3: P2, YO, SSK, k2tog, YO 2x, SSK, k2tog, YO, p2, TC6B, TC6F, p2, YO, SSK, k2tog, YO 2x, SSK, k2tog, YO, p2.
Round 4: P2, k3, p1, k4, p2, k4, p4, k4, p2, k3, p1, k4, p2.
Round 5: P2, [k2tog, YO 2x, SSK] 2x, p2, k4, p4, k4, p2, [k2tog, YO 2x, SSK] 2x, p2.
Round 6: P2, k1, p1, k3, p1, k2, p2, k4, p4, k4, p2, k1, p1, k3, p1, k2, p2.
Round 7: C2F, p2, k2tog, YO 2x, SSK, p2, TC6B, k2tog, YO 2x, SSK, TC6F, p2, k2tog, YO 2x, SSK, p2, C2B.

Round 8: K2, p2, k1, p1, k2, p2, k4, p2, k1, p1, k2, p2, k4, p2, k1, p1, k2, p2, k2.
Round 9: K2, [p2, YO, SSK, k2tog, YO, p2, k4] 2x, p2, YO, SSK, k2tog, YO, p2, k2.
Round 10: K2, [p2, k4] 5x, p2, k2.
Round 11: C4F, p4, TC6B, YO, SSK, k2tog, YO 2x, SSK, k2tog, YO, TC6F, p4, C4B.
Round 12: K4, p4, k4, p2, k3, p1, k4, p2, k4, p4, k4.
Round 13: K4, p4, k4, p2, [k2tog, YO 2x, SSK] 2x, p2, k4, p4, k4.
Round 14: K4, p4, k4, p2, k1, p1, k3, p1, k2, p2, k4, p4, k4.
Round 15: TC6F, TC6B, [k2tog, YO 2x, SSK] 3x, TC6F, TC6B.
Round 16: P2, k8, p2, k1, p1, [k3, p1] 2x, k2, p2, k8, p2.
Round 17: P2, k8, p2, YO, SSK, [k2tog, YO twice, SSK] 2x, k2tog, YO, p2, k8, p2.
Round 18: P2, k8, p2, [k3, p1] 2x, k4, p2, k8, p2.
Round 19: TC6B, TC6F, p2, YO, SSK, k2tog, YO 2x, SSK, k2tog, YO, p2, TC6B, TC6F.
Round 20: K4, p4, k4, p2, k3, p1, k4, p2, k4, p4, k4.
Round 21: K4, p4, k4, p2, [k2tog, YO twice, SSK] 2x, p2, k4, p4, k4.
Round 22: K4, p4, k4, p2, k1, p1, k3, p1, k2, p2, k4, p4, k4.

Round 23: T4B, k2tog, YO 2x, SSK, TC6F, p2, k2tog, YO 2x, SSK, p2, TC6B, k2tog, YO 2x, SSK, T4F.

Round 24: K2, p2, k1, p1, [k2, p2, k4, p2, k1, p1] 2x, k2, p2, k2.

Round 25: K2, p2, [YO, SSK, k2tog, YO, p2, k4, p2] 2x, YO, SSK, k2tog, YO, p2, k2.

Round 26: K2, [p2, k4] 5x, p2, k2.

Round 27: T2B, YO, SSK, k2tog, YO 2x, SSK, k2tog, YO, TC6F, p4, TC6B, YO, SSK, k2tog, YO 2x, SSK, k2tog, YO, T2F.

Round 28: P2, k3, p1, k4, p2, k4, p4, k4, p2, k3, p1, k4, p2.

Round 29: P2, [k2tog, YO 2x, SSK] 2x, p2, k4, p4, k4, p2, [k2tog, YO 2x, SSK] 2x, p2.

Round 30: P2, k1, p1, k3, p1, k2, p2, k4, p4, k4, p2, k1, p1, k3, p1, k2, p2.

Round 31: [K2tog, YO 2x, SSK] 3x, TC6F, TC6B, [k2tog, YO 2x, SSK] 3x.

Round 32: K1, p1, [k3, p1] 2x, k2, p2, k8, p2, k1, p1, [k3, p1] 2x, k2.

Heel

Work across instep stitches in pattern. Drop MC but do not break. Join CC. The heel turn will now be worked back-and-forth in CC over the 36 heel stitches.

Shape Bottom of Heel

Row 1 (RS): K35, W&T.

Row 2 (WS): P34, W&T.

Row 3: Knit to stitch before wrapped stitch (do not knit any wrapped stitches), W&T.

Row 4: Purl to stitch before wrapped stitch (do not purl any wrapped stitches), W&T.

Repeat Rows 3-4 an additional 10x – there are now 12 wrapped stitches on either side of 12 unwrapped center stitches.

Shape Top of Heel

Row 1 (RS): Knit to first wrapped stitch (do not knit across any wrapped stitches), lift wrap RS, turn.

Row 2 (WS): Sl1, purl to first wrapped stitch (do not purl across any wrapped stitches), lift wrap WS, turn.

Row 3: Sl1, knit to next wrapped stitch (just past the stitch unwrapped on the previous RS row), lift wrap RS, turn.

Row 4: Sl1, purl to next wrapped stitch (just past the stitch unwrapped on the previous WS row), lift wrap WS, turn.

Repeat Rows 3-4 an additional 9x – a single wrapped stitch remains on either side of heel. Break CC.

Next Row: With MC and larger needles, sl1, knit to last wrapped stitch, lift wrap RS but do not turn. You should be at the beginning of the instep stitches.

Next Round: Work instep stitches in pattern as established, noting pattern round #; lift wrap RS, knit to end of heel stitches.

Leg

Begin working all stitches in *Diamond Cables for Leg* as follows (or from chart on p. 157), starting on the next pattern round # as worked for instep (i.e. if last instep round worked was 1, start leg pattern on Round 2). Work even in pattern until leg measures approximately 5-1/2" from top of heel, ending with Round 1 or Round 17 of pattern.

Note: When working cables across the beginning of round, such as on Round 8, you should not be moving the beginning of round location. The same number of stitches should remain on each needle, just swap their locations so you can complete the cables.

Diamond Cables for Leg

(over 72 stitches and 32 rounds)

Round 1: *YO, SSK, [k2tog, YO 2x, SSK] 2x, k2tog, YO, p2, k8, p2; repeat from * 2x more.

Round 2: *[K3, p1] 2x, k4, p2, k8, p2; repeat from * 2x more.

Round 3: *P2, YO, SSK, k2tog, YO 2x, SSK, k2tog, YO, p2, TC6B, TC6F; repeat from * 2x more.

Round 4: *P2, k3, p1, k4, p2, k4, p4, k4; repeat from * 2x more.

Round 5: *P2, [k2tog, YO 2x, SSK] 2x, p2, k4, p4, k4; repeat from * 2x more.

Round 6: *P2, k1, p1, k3, p1, k2, p2, k4, p4, k4; repeat from * 2x more.

Round 7: P4, *k2tog, YO 2x, SSK, p2, TC6B, k2tog, YO 2x, SSK, TC6F, p2; repeat from *, k2tog, YO 2x, SSK, p2, TC6B, k2tog, YO 2x, SSK, TC6F using 2 stitches from beginning of next round.

Round 8 (worked on remaining 70 stitches after TC6F at end of Round 7): *P2, k1, p1, k2, p2, k4; repeat from * an additional 4x, p2, k1, p1, k2, p2, k2.

Round 9: K2, *p2, YO, SSK, k2tog, YO, p2, k4; repeat from * an additional 4x, p2, YO, SSK, k2tog, YO, p2, k2.

Round 10: K2, [p2, k4] 11x, p2, k2.

Round 11: K2, p6, *TC6B, YO, SSK, k2tog, YO 2x, SSK, k2tog, YO, TC6F, p4; repeat from *, TC6B, YO, SSK, k2tog, YO 2x, SSK, k2tog, YO, TC6F using 4 stitches from beginning of next round.

Round 12 (worked on remaining 68 stitches after TC6F at end of Round 11): *P4, k4, p2, k3, p1, k4, p2, k4; repeat from * once more, p4, k4, p2, k3, p1, k4, p2.

Round 13: *K4, p4, k4, p2, [k2tog, YO twice, SSK] 2x, p2; repeat from * twice more.

Round 14: *K4, p4, k4, p2, k1, p1, k3, p1, k2, p2; repeat from * twice more.

Round 15: *TC6F, TC6B, [k2tog, YO 2x, SSK] 3x; repeat from * twice more.

Round 16: *P2, k8, p2, k1, p1, [k3, p1] 2x, k2; repeat from * twice more.

Round 17: *P2, k8, p2, YO, SSK, [k2tog, YO 2x, SSK] 2x, k2tog, YO; repeat from * twice more.

Round 18: *P2, k8, p2, [k3, p1] 2x, k4; repeat from * twice more.

Round 19: *TC6B, TC6F, p2, YO, SSK, k2tog, YO 2x, SSK, k2tog, YO, p2; repeat from * twice more.

Round 20: *K4, p4, k4, p2, k3, p1, k4, p2; repeat from * twice more.

Round 21: *K4, p4, k4, p2, [k2tog, YO 2x, SSK] 2x, p2; repeat from * twice more.

Round 22: *K4, p4, k4, p2, k1, p1, k3, p1, k2, p2; repeat from * twice more.

Round 23: K4, *k2tog, YO 2x, SSK, TC6F, p2, k2tog, YO 2x, SSK, p2, TC6B; repeat from *, k2tog, YO 2x, SSK, TC6F, p2, k2tog, YO 2x, SSK, p2, TC6B using 4 stitches from beginning of next round.

Round 24 (worked on remaining 68 stitches after TC6B at end of Round 23): *K1, p1, k2, p2, k4, p2; repeat from * an additional 4x, k1, p1, k2, p2, k2.

Round 25: K2, *p2, YO, SSK, k2tog, YO, p2, k4; repeat from * an additional 4x, p2, YO, SSK, k2tog, YO, p2, k2.

Round 26: K2, [p2, k4] 11x, p2, k2.

Round 27: K2, *YO, SSK, k2tog, YO, 2x, SSK, k2tog, YO, TC6F, p4, TC6B; repeat from *, YO, SSK, k2tog, YO 2x, SSK, k2tog, YO, TC6F, p4, TC6B using 2 stitches from beginning of next round.

Round 28 (worked on remaining 70 stitches after TC6F at end of Round 27): *K3, p1, k4, p2, k4, p4, k4, p2; repeat from *, k3, p1, k4, p2, k4, p4, k4.

Round 29: *P2, [k2tog, YO 2x, SSK] 2x, p2, k4, p4, k4; repeat from * twice more.

Round 30: *P2, k1, p1, k3, p1, k2, p2, k4, p4, k4; repeat from * twice more.

Round 31: *[k2tog, YO 2x, SSK] 3x, TC6F, TC6B; repeat from * twice more.

Round 32: *K1, p1, [k3, p1] 2x, k2, p2, k8, p2; repeat from * twice more.

Cuff

Break MC. Join CC.

Note: If you are having trouble with your cuff flaring out, decrease 8 or 10 stitches evenly spaced around Round 1 to help eliminate any looseness.

Round 1: Knit.
Round 2: Purl.
Round 3: *YO, k2tog; repeat from * to end of round.
Round 4: Purl.

Bind off all stitches loosely as follows: K1, *YO, k1, using tip of left needle, pass 2nd and 3rd stitches on right needle over 1st stitch on right needle (one stitch remains on right needle); repeat from * until all stitches are bound off. Fasten off.

Finishing
Weave in any remaining ends, dampen socks and lay flat to block or use sock blockers.

Diamond Cables for Instep

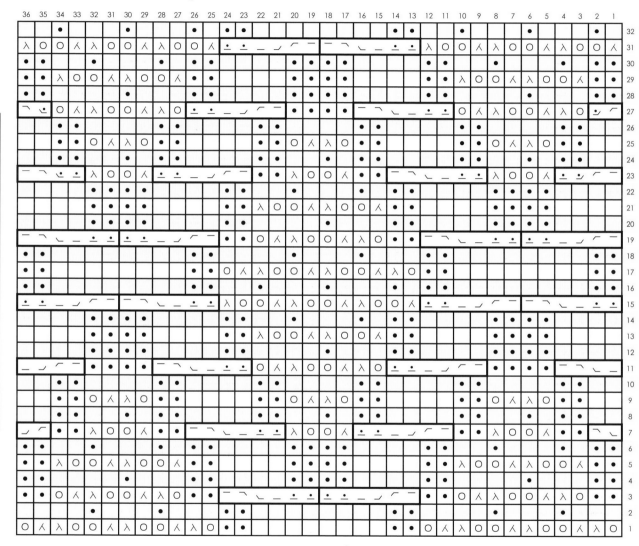

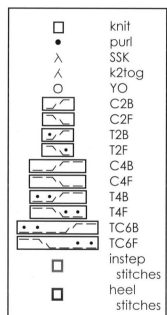

□	knit	
•	purl	
⅄	SSK	
⋏	k2tog	
O	YO	
	C2B	
	C2F	
	T2B	
	T2F	
	C4B	
	C4F	
	T4B	
	T4F	
	TC6B	
	TC6F	
□	instep stitches	
□	heel stitches	

Diamond Cables for Leg

(see p. 156 for chart key)

Materials:

Approximately 400 yards of fingering-weight yarn. *Sample uses Lorna's Laces Shepherd Sock (100% superwash merino wool) in 'Retro Soda'.*

US1 (2.25mm) needles or size needed to obtain gauge

Yarn needle

Gauge:

8-1/2 stitches/12 rounds per inch in stockinette stitch

Size:

Foot circumference = approximately 8"

Soda Fountain

Designer's Notes:

When I saw this colorway, which the talented ladies at Lorna's Laces designed especially for me, I was immediately reminded of the fruit-flavored sodas I loved as a kid - grape, orange and root beer.

While these strong shades make a high-impact yarn, they also have all the properties that can make that yarn a real headache to deal with. Instead of trying to fight with the contrast, I opted to use horizontal bands of smocking to add interest to a relatively simple ribbing. Linen stitch heel flaps always work very well with strong colorways like this one.

Keeping it simple doesn't always mean boring, and an added benefit to this relatively uncomplicated ribbing pattern is that it knits up in a flash.

Special Abbreviations and Techniques for This Pattern

small smock: Sl4, bring yarn to front and slip those same 4 stitches back to left needle, bring yarn to back wrapping working yarn loosely around the base of these 4 stitches to complete the smocking; repeat from * once more, k4 (the 4 smocked stitches).

large smock: Sl6, bring yarn to front and slip those same 6 stitches back to left needle, bring yarn to back wrapping working yarn loosely around the base of these 4 stitches to complete the smocking; repeat from * once more, k6 (the 6 smocked stitches).

Note: You may need to experiment with the tension of the wrapped yarn, so that it is not pulling the ribbing in too tightly but at the same time is not looser than the stitches and saggy.

Leg

Cast on 72 stitches and divide them over dpns or circular needles as follows:

- If using dpns, place 22 stitches on each of needles 1 and 3, and 14 stitches on each of needles 2 and 4.
- If using circular needle(s), place 36 stitches on each needle.

The first 36 stitches of the round are the instep stitches and the last 36 stitches are the heel stitches. Join stitches into round being careful not to twist.

Round 1: *P1, k2, p2, k4, [p2, k2] 4x, p2, k4, p2, k2, p1; repeat from * across heel stitches.
Repeat Round 1 an additional 7x.

Begin working *Smocked Rib Pattern* as follows (or from chart on p. 162) across all stitches:

Smocked Rib Pattern

(over a multiple of 36 stitches and 12 rounds)
Round 1: *P1, k2, p2, small smock, p2, k2, p10, k2, p2, small smock, p2, k2, p1; repeat from *.
Round 2-4: *P1, k2, p2, k4, p2, k2, p10, k2, p2, k4, p2, k2, p1; repeat from *.
Round 5: *P1, k2, p2, k4, p2, k2, p2, large smock, p2, k2, p2, k4, p2, k2, p1; repeat from *.
Round 6: *P1, k2, p2, k4, [p2, k2] 4x, p2, k4, p2, k2, p1; repeat from *.
Round 7: *P1, k2, p2, small smock, p2, k2, p2, k6, p2, k2, p2, small smock, p2, k2, p1; repeat from *.
Round 8: Repeat Round 6.
Round 9: *P1, k2, p2, k4, p2, k2, p2, k6, p2, k2, p2, k4, p2, k2, p1; repeat from *.
Round 10: Repeat Round 6.
Round 11: Repeat Round 9.
Round 12: Repeat Round 6.

Repeat Rounds 1-12 until leg measures approximately 5" from start (or desired length to top of heel flap), ending with Round 2 of pattern.

Heel Flap

Work across instep stitches in pattern. The heel flap will then be worked back-and-forth over the 36 heel stitches.
Row 1 (RS): Sl1, [k1, sl1-wyif] 17x, k1, turn.
Row 2: Sl1, purl to end of row, turn.
Row 3: Sl1, [sl1-wyif, k1] 17x, k1, turn.
Row 4: Sl1, purl to end of row, turn.
Repeat Rows 1-4 an additional 6x.

Turn Heel

Row 1 (RS): Sl1, k18, SSK, k1, turn.
Row 2: Sl1, p3, p2tog, p1, turn.
Row 3: Sl1, knit to stitch before gap formed by previous row's turn, SSK, k1, turn.
Row 4: Sl1, purl to stitch before gap formed by previous row's turn, p2tog, p1, turn.
Repeat Rows 3-4 until all heel flap stitches have been worked. 20 heel stitches remain.

Shape Gusset

Knit across the 20 heel stitches. Working up the side of the heel flap with the same needle, pu 14 stitches. Work instep stitches in pattern as established. Working down the other side of the heel flap with an empty dpn or empty end of second circular needle, pu 14 stitches. 48 heel stitches.

If using dpns, knit the first 10 stitches from the second heel needle onto the first so there are an equal number of heel stitches on each needle.

To get back to the beginning of the round, knit to the end of the heel stitches.

Round 1: Work instep stitches in pattern as established; knit to last 3 heel stitches, k2tog, k1.

Round 2: Work instep stitches in pattern as established; k1, SSK, knit to end of heel stitches.

Repeat Rounds 1-2 an additional 5x. 36 heel stitches, 72 total stitches.

Foot

Continue to work instep stitches in pattern as established and heel stitches in stockinette stitch until foot from start of heel turn to needles measures approximately 2" less than desired finished bottom-of-foot length.

Toe

Round 1: Knit.

Round 2: *K1, SSK, knit to last 3 instep stitches, k2tog, k1; repeat from * across heel stitches. 68 stitches.

Repeat Rounds 1-2 an additional 10x. 28 stitches. Then, repeat Round 1 only an additional 3x. 16 stitches.

Cut yarn, leaving a 14-16" tail. Graft toe closed using Kitchener Stitch.

Finishing

Weave in any remaining ends, dampen socks and lay flat to block or use sock blockers.

Smocked Rib Pattern

36	35	34	33	32	31	30	29	28	27	26	25	24	23	22	21	20	19	18	17	16	15	14	13	12	11	10	9	8	7	6	5	4	3	2	1	
•			•	•					•	•			•	•		•	•				•	•			•	•					•	•			•	12
•			•	•					•	•			•	•							•	•			•	•					•	•			•	11
•			•	•					•	•			•	•			•	•			•	•			•	•					•	•			•	10
•			•	•					•	•			•	•							•	•			•	•					•	•			•	9
•			•	•					•	•			•	•		•	•				•	•			•	•					•	•			•	8
•			•	•		═══			•	•			•	•							•	•			•	•		═══			•	•			•	7
•			•	•					•	•			•	•			•	•			•	•			•	•					•	•			•	6
•			•	•					•	•			•	•		════					•	•			•	•					•	•			•	5
•			•	•					•	•			•	•	•	•	•	•	•	•	•	•			•	•					•	•			•	4
•			•	•					•	•			•	•	•	•	•	•	•	•	•	•			•	•					•	•			•	3
•			•	•	•				•	•			•	•	•	•	•	•	•	•	•	•			•	•					•	•			•	2
•			•	•		═══			•	•			•	•	•	•	•	•	•	•	•	•			•	•		═══			•	•			•	1

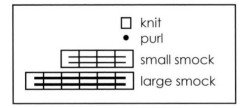

□ knit
• purl
small smock
large smock

Dyer Profiles

Owner: Anne Morrow

Date Established: 2009

Location: Vancouver, Washington

Favorite Color: coral pink

Favorite Movies: *Cool Hand Luke*, *Doctor Zhivago* and *Cat on a Hot Tin Roof*

Featured Yarn: Luxe B

Colorway: *The World Is My Oyster*

Inspiration: "I like colorways that look slightly different depending on the light. This colorway is somewhere between a lavender and silver with hints of pink and blue. It reminds me of oyster shells, which led to the name choice. "

Alpha B Yarn

Anyone who has ever met Anne Morrow knows she is funny, irreverent and doesn't take herself too seriously. The fact that she creates captivating yarn is a bonus!

Anne began her career as a hand-dyer in 2009. A friend of hers was dyeing yarn, and Anne thought she might also enjoy it. After spending some time reading about dyeing and learning the ins and outs from her friend, she gave it a try. When describing her first dyeing experience, Anne wrote "it was a complete disaster. The yarn was a color not found in nature and was slightly felted. I'm surprised I even tried again."

However, she perservered and, through trial, error, and more than a little hard work, developed a palette and product line that she is proud to put her name on.

Anne began selling her yarn after showing it to some out-of-town friends during Sock Summit 2009. With time left on the meter after visiting Portland, Oregon, yarn shop Knit Purl, Anne opened the back of her car to reveal the yarn. As her friends were choosing the colors they liked, Anne asked if they thought anyone would buy her yarn. The answer was a resounding "yes!" and Alpha B Yarn became a reality.

When asked about her current dye studio, Anne replied "You're joking, right? I dye in my garage. The floor resembles a Jackson Pollack painting after several mishaps. One time, I dropped a 1500 ml container of bright blue. Luckily, it was summer and I used a hose to clean the floor. Unfortunately, my feet were bright blue for several days."

What Sets This Company Apart
Bright, unique semi-solid colors on luxury base yarns.

Contact Info
www.alphabyarn.etsy.com

"I dye a little irreverence into every skein."

Shalimar Yarns

Kristi Johnson, owner of Shalimar Yarns, has been submersed in the fiber arts her entire life. Her mother, a very creative and talented woman, taught Kristi all about knitting, needlesmithing and sewing as she was growing up.

Kristi spent a lot of time in yarn shops with her mother, which gave her an edge when she and her partner, Paul, decided to open their own yarn shop, Eleganza Yarns, in Frederick, Maryland. Before opening the shop, she had a long career in the organic and sustainability aspects of the produce industry.

Shalimar Yarns grew out of a desire to diversify the offerings in her yarn shop a few years after opening. When Kristi started dyeing yarn, she had no idea that she would love it as much as she does or that it would grow into the thriving wholesale business it is now.

In the past year, Kristi has closed her yarn shop and now focuses full-time on Shalimar Yarns, which has grown considerably. She tends to do most of her dyeing in the morning, when she is freshest, then spends the afternoons working on more focused, business-related tasks. Kristi counts herself pretty lucky to have such a remarkably stimulating, fiber-filled life.

What Sets This Company Apart

Kristi feels that she has a true partnership with her customers. They are helping her do what she loves and she is doing everything she can to make sure they are successful. For example, she has had pattern support for the yarn line since the very start, including patterns that are free to her wholesale customers.

Contact Info

www.shalimaryarns.com
5917 Boyers Mill Road
New Market, MD 21774
shalimaryarns@aol.com

"Shalimar is an extension of the passions in my life and it is wonderful to be able to combine them on a daily basis."

Owner: Kristi Johnson

Date Established: 2006

Location: Frederick, Maryland

Favorite Color: red

Favorite Book: *A is for Annabelle* by Tasha Tudor

Hobby: doll making

Featured Yarn: Zoe Sock

Colorway: *Sprout*

Inspiration: "The green was so springy and happy that it just begged to be named *Sprout*."

Curious Creek Fibers

Owner: Kristine Brooks

Date Established: 2004

Location: San Diego, California

Favorite Movies: *The Princess Bride* and *The Philadelphia Story*

Hobbies: riding motorcycles, weaving, spinning, watercolor painting, reading

Featured Yarn: Serengeti

Colorways: *Old Head of Kinsale* and *Sunrise on Daffodils*

Inspiration: *Old Head of Kinsale* was designed for a Woolgirl sock club selection in 2009, inspired by photos Woolgirl owner Jennifer Jett took in Old Kinsale, Ireland. *Sunrise on Daffodils* was designed with Kristine's grandmother, Grace Brooks Leahy, in mind. Her favorite color was yellow, and she always had every color of daffodil in her garden.

Kristine Brooks was raised by a wonderfully inventive mother who was a fiber artist in her own right. She "had an amazing gift for color" and was pairing different textures, styles and colors in her sewing projects long before it was fashionable.

Another important presence in Kristine's life is her husband Phil, a scientist, who designed dyeing tables that are ergonomically perfect for Kristine but still look beautiful in their 1912 Craftsman-style home.

When Kristine started to think about making a career change in 2002, the influence of both of these folks can be seen in her approach. At that time, she was still running her first business, K Brooks Consulting, which provided estate management services to affluent southern Californians.

In 2002 she took a dyeing class that she found fun, but a bit haphazard. She decided to apply the scientific method to her dyeing by changing one thing at a time to see the cause and effect. This produced repeatable colorways that she found pleasing.

She then took her idea for Curious Creek Fibers through a formal research and development phase, as well as a test market phase, before opening for business in 2004. Within six months, she was able to leave her old job behind and concentrate full time on Curious Creek Fibers.

What Sets This Company Apart

Kristine uses many different dye techniques to approach her colorways, each one named to tell a story with color. "The idea is to dye the yarn in an 'organic mixture' of colors, making nearly every stitch a different color experience, no matter how subtle or bold."

Contact Info

www.curiouscreek.com
3070 Palm Street
San Diego, CA 92104
619/280.2404

"Each batch of yarn is a little piece of me."

The Sweet Sheep

Michelle Szeghalmi-Shirley has a compulsive need to create. She sees something and thinks "I need to make that". Several years ago, she found herself buying lots of yarn and felt a strong desire to try her hand at dyeing. She purchased some undyed skeins and set about teaching herself to dye one summer in her parents' garage. Her first attempts were very bright, but she loved them, and so a new indie dyer was created.

Over the years, Michelle's tastes and techniques have changed and expanded. She now purposely dyes outside of her color comfort zone, and tries to make yarn that expresses what she is feeling on the day she dyes it.

Her studio, which was built by her husband, contains a variety of dyes and equipment, including crock pots, burners, microwaves, steamers, and a few toaster ovens. Based on Michelle's mood or the particular end result she is looking for, she will use different combinations of tools, techniques and dyes.

Michelle's dye studio is open 24 hours a day so that she can work whenever the mood strikes. She loves having the freedom to express herself at any time. This openness to her creative process is one reason why many of The Sweet Sheep's colorways are one of a kind and not repeatable.

What Sets This Company Apart

Michelle's yarns represent artistic expression for her, and she approaches her dyeing process like an artist. This is reflected in her use of colors and yarn bases she loves and knows will be pleasing to other fiber artists.

Contact Info

www.thesweetsheep.com

"My colorways are my art."

Owner: Michelle Szeghalmi-Shirley

Date Established: 2006

Location: Newcastle, Ontario

Favorite Color: varies among purple, pink, red and blue

Favorite Movie: more action flicks than chick flicks

Hobby: spinning

Featured Yarn: Sweet Socks Tight Twist

Colorway: *Love Rocks*

Inspiration: *"Love Rocks* was born out of an inspiration for a soft slow marbling yarn that would express my comfortable and content mood."

Owner: Cheryl Schaefer

Date Established: 1992

Location: Interlaken, New York

Number of Employees: 6

Favorite Colors: olive green and purple

Favorite Movies: *How Green Was My Valley; Now, Voyager;* and *Mrs. Miniver*

Hobbies: gardening and crazy quilt embroidery

Featured Yarn: Nichole

Colorway: *Chamomile*

Inspiration: "*Chamomile* is one of our new line of Subtly Solid colors. These colors have gentle variation throughout the skein without any strong lines or changes of color so they work up to look 'hand-dyed' but still maintain a monochromatic feel."

The Schaefer Yarn Co.

"It all began in California in 1979 after I had imported variegated yarn from Israel to sell. It was supposed to be merino and turned out to be rug yarn. Believing I could do it myself but knowing nothing about dyeing, I set about finding fleece and a mill to spin it into a homespun. After much experimenting in the enameled bin of an old refrigerator, I learned what not to do and eventually could control the results. I was certainly artistic, but painting and dyeing are worlds apart. The only thing painterly was my approach to dyeing, and I coined the phrase 'hand-painted yarns' long before it was adopted by the hand-dyeing industry.

"Once the yarn was consistent, and consistently beautiful, I began to sell it. I moved back east and started Dyed In The Wool in New York, my hometown. I knew even less about business than I did about dyeing back then, but I needed flexible hours as a single parent of a disabled child, so I just followed my instincts.

"While that business was successful, the partnerships involved were not; my association with it ended in 1986 and the company eventually folded. I created another yarn dyeing venture with my new husband, Erich, in upstate New York.

"The business eventually took over the entire house, barn and garage and we needed a different place to live. Today it takes 6 people to produce the yarn and we live 400 feet away in 'The House That Yarn Built' of which we are shamelessly proud."
- *Cheryl Schaefer*

What Sets This Company Apart
Consistent quality in both colorways and fiber content.

Contact Info
www.schaeferyarn.com
3514 Kellys Corners Rd
Interlaken, NY 14847
607/532.9452

"*Even after 30 years, I doubt any of my family can believe I have been this successful in business.*"

Miss Babs

Babs Ausherman was born into a large, very creative and entrepreneurial family. It was only natural that she learned to knit when she was six, having already mastered sewing. It also made sense for her to go to culinary school in western North Carolina in her early 20's and then briefly own an ice cream shop. Eventually, Babs joined the family insurance business, where she learned a lot about people and running a company.

When Babs was 35, her mother died after a long bout with breast cancer. This had a profound effect on her life. It was at this time that she realized she should not wait to do what she wanted, but should just start working toward it. She went back to school, earned her MBA and eventually taught marketing at Appalachian State University. She also developed and ran an online book selling business and baked for a local coffee shop, allowing her to keep her feet in the entrepreneurial world.

Then, one fateful day, Babs took a natural dye workshop at a local state park. It was outside using wood fires and just felt right to her. She came home from the event and immersed herself in the world of dyeing. She bought inexpensive wool over the internet along with acid dyes, plant materials and books about dyeing.

Now she spends very long days, starting at about four a.m., working in her dye studio, which is just under 1000 square feet. Both Babs and her husband are grateful to the business that has allowed her to support her family and do the things she loves.

What Sets This Company Apart
Miss Babs has a very broad palette of colors, both monochromatic and variegated, that coordinate and span the color spectrum.

Contact Info
www.missbabs.com
PO Box 78
Mountain City, TN 37683
423/727.0670

"Fiber is elemental to my life as a woman and as an artist."

Owner: Babs Ausherman

Date Established: 2003

Location: Mountain City, Tennessee

Number of Employees: 4

Favorite Colors: green and black

Favorite Authors: Tolstoy, Harding, Austen and Joyce

Hobbies: spinning, knitting single socks

Featured Yarn: "Yummy" Monochrome Sock & Baby Yarn

Colorway: *French Marigold*

Inspiration: This colorway was named after the French marigold flower. "We like to name things after flora and fauna. That adds an additional dimension for the knitter as they work with the yarn."

Elemental Affects

Owner: *Jeane deCoster*

Date Established: 2005

Location: Desert Hot Springs, California

Favorite Color: Used to be beige, now all colors, depending on mood

Favorite Books: 'dime' novels, mostly romance and mystery

Hobbies: life, but also weaving, spinning, collecting beads and buttons, sewing

Featured Yarn: Natural Shetland Fingering

Colorways: *Forest Moss, Musket, Lime Juice, Lichen, Yellow* and *Fawn*

When Jeane deCoster found out she was being downsized after more than 20 years in high tech, she took it as a sign that it was time to do something totally different. She has always been fascinated with all things related to the fiber arts, knitting and sewing since she was a child. She holds a bachelor's degree in fashion design and has worked in the fashion industry.

Around the time her high tech career was ending, Jeane started to research hand-dyeing, reading everything she could find on the subject. She took classes from every source she could find, including a remote learning offering from New Zealand, PRO Chemical & Dye workshops, and even a two week course from renowned textiles expert Allen Fannin.

When she felt she had a good grasp of the subject, she tried to buy an existing yarn company. That deal fell through, but she took away from the experience the realization that she was ready to start her own company.

Around this time, Jeane learned of a Shetland wool producer in the U.S. who did not have a way to get its wool to market. She contracted with them to buy their wool and found a commercial mill in the U.S. that turned it into an exquisite fingering weight yarn for her. She now dyes that yarn into a rainbow of solid colors suitable for everything from fine Fair Isle Sweaters to socks.

Jeane was clear from the beginning that her venture was a business and it needed to support her. Her approach has been methodical and well researched, but in the end she still touches every skein of yarn she sells and gets to spend her days doing exactly what she wants.

What Sets This Company Apart
In addition to making their own domestic, breed-specific yarns, Elemental Affects produces a wide range of shades by dyeing over the natural colors of the fleece.

Contact Info
www.elementalaffects.com

"Colors are simply the emotion you are trying to evoke."

Pico(t)

In 2005, Stevanie Pico found herself working for a Portland, Oregon, yarn shop called Abundant Yarn and Dyeworks. The owner at the time, who had a Waldorf background, took all of her employees to a day of natural dye training in the gardens of a local woman.

While there, the employees were given unrestricted access to the gardens. While Stevanie was dumping her exhausted dye pots, she noticed a fire pit with benches and cleared paths around it. She asked the hostess about this space, and was surprised to hear that the woman had lost a 4 year old daughter years before and this was her place of burial. She went on to explain that "we gather here with our friends and family - surrounded by the garden - and are reminded that life continues".

For Stevanie, this continuation of life is what natural dyeing is all about. She gives leftover food, roots, plants, wood and other natural materials a continued life by using them to dye natural yarns and fibers that are enjoyed by knitters everywhere.

Dyeing with natural materials is very different from dyeing with acids or other dyes. Each material requires its own timeframe, from a few minutes to multiple days. Because of this, when you visit the Pico(t) studio it is always littered with pots full of yarns in different dyeing stages. You never know what will greet you on the overhead drying racks, but you can be sure it will be unlike anything you've ever seen before.

What Sets This Company Apart
Vibrant and unique yarns and fibers dyed with various combinations of natural and acid dyes that provide colorways like no other.

Contact Info
www.picohanddyed.com

"...my friends, family and special places inspire me to try to recreate certain feelings or moods; some yarns are like showing the knitter an album of photos"

Owner: Stevanie Pico

Date Established: 2011, formerly part of Pico Accuardi Dyeworks

Location: Portland, Oregon

Favorite Color: Green

Favorite Movies: *The Big Lebowski* and *Eternal Sunshine of the Spotless Mind*

Hobbies: salsa dancing, singing, stalking Leonard Nimoy with her friend Larissa

Featured Yarn: La Libera

Colorway: *Gwendolyn*

Inspiration: "A day or two after I dyed it, my friend Gwen saw it and flipped out. Gwen always describes finding beautiful yarn on the shelf the same way you would describe falling in love at first sight. I named it after her full name, Gwendolyn."

Owner: Sharon Spence

Date Established: 2008

Location: Hillsboro, Oregon

Favorite Color: green

Favorite Movies: *Blazing Saddles* and *This is Spinal Tap*

Favorite Author: Stephen King

Featured Yarn: 100% Merino Sock

Colorway: *Crush*

Inspiration: "I decided to call it *Crush* to go with the recurring heavy metal theme in Stitchjones, and also because it's orange."

Stitchjones

On a fortuitous day in mid-2007, Sharon Spence, founder of Stitchjones Hand-Dyed Yarn and Fiber, decided to try her hand at dyeing some yarn at home with Kool-Aid brand drink and instructions she found on the internet. She was, in a word, hooked. She bought several dyeing books, including *The Twisted Sisters Sock Book*, some professional dyes, and took off.

From the start, Sharon was interested in finding a way to express herself artistically. The idea of leaving the 'rat race' while doing so was also an attractive possibility. She started by offering her yarn on Etsy.com and quickly followed with a wholesale line.

Sharon's eclectic and exciting color sense, along with the sales training she received as a Mary Kay representative, have helped to establish her as an indie dyer with exciting offerings and excellent customer service.

Recently, Sharon became the proud owner of a local knit shop, Kathy's Knit Corner, in Forest Grove, Oregon. This has offered Sharon the opportunity to immerse herself even further in the fiber arts. The store has a space which Sharon has converted into a dyeing studio for Stitchjones, allowing her to move the business out of her kitchen. Her family is quite excited about this development!

What Sets This Company Apart
Deep, rich, saturated colors, with colorways named after rock music themes.

Contact Info
www.stitchjones.com
sharon@stitchjones.com

"There is so much more to the business than just dyeing, and I devote considerably more time to it than I would if I were working for someone else."

Hazel Knits

From the moment Wendee Shulsen learned to knit, she knew she had a passion for yarn. She couldn't get enough of the colors and textures, so she decided to get a job in her local yarn shop to earn some extra yarn money. While there, she started to play around with dyeing in order to fulfill various customer requests. She enjoyed it so much, she decided to make it her full-time career.

Wendee did not start her yarn dyeing venture unprepared. Wendee grew up on a farm, where she was instilled with a knowledge of the hard work required to make your dreams a reality. Before starting Hazel Knits, she'd spent several years in retail and customer service, including 10 years as a production manager and inventor for a board game company. During this time, she learned various color and design techniques as well as what it takes to get a product to market.

Now Wendee enjoys long but rewarding days in a home studio that is filled with light. She has separate rooms for dyeing, drying, and skeining and shipping. She also has a storage area

for both finished and undyed product. However, Hazel Knits still spills over into the rest of her house on occasion.

As with so many people lucky enough to make a living through their art, this blending of the personal and the professional (not just with space, but in all aspects of her life), is reflected in the beauty of her final product.

What Sets This Company Apart
A clear, bright color palette and custom spun base yarns that are unique to Hazel Knits.

Contact Info
www.hazelknits.com
wendee@hazelknits.com

"Many 16 hour days and a few tons of wool later, and I'm still loving it!"

Owner: Wendee Shulsen

Date Established: 2007

Location: Seattle, Washington

Favorite Color: orange

Favorite Movie: *A Christmas Story*

Favorite Author: David Sedaris

Hobbies: rock climbing, sewing, making things grow, and hula hooping

Featured Yarn: Artisan Sock

Colorway: *Wheatberry*

Inspiration: Wendee's father was a grain farmer. "The wheat brought home the bacon!"

Mountain Colors

Owners: Leslie Taylor & Diana McKay

Date Established: 1992

Location: Corvallis, Montana

Number of Employees: 10

Favorite Colors: Leslie - teal, burgundy; Diana - red, blue, purple and all others

Hobbies: weaving, spinning

Featured Yarn: Crazyfoot

Colorway: *Northwind*

Inspiration: All color names are based on colors of the Rocky Mountain west: rivers, mountains, plants and animals.

When their children were small, Leslie Taylor and Diana McKay were looking for something to do that would provide a little extra cash while leaving them with enough time and flexibility to regularly volunteer in their children's schools. At the time, their small rural community didn't have much to offer, so they had to get creative!

After they gave a dyeing demonstration at a local fiber festival where their hand-dyed yarns were well received, Diana and Leslie decided to see if selling yarn would fill their needs. They started dyeing in Diana's kitchen, then moved into a commercial space in Stevensville, Montana. After several years of growth, during which time their children worked and grew along side them, they relocated to their current space in Corvallis, Montana.

Even as their business has grown, many things have remained the same. For example, each skein of yarn sold by Mountain Colors is still hand-tied and hand-painted.

Mountain Colors grew out of the desire of two women to be available to, yet still provide for, their families. This family focus is still very much a part of the Mountain Colors culture, where all employees are encouraged to take time off for important family events and spend time with their children.

What Sets This Company Apart
Strong, distinctive colors on a wide range of animal fibers along with outstanding, personal customer service.

Contact Info
www.mountaincolors.com
info@mountaincolors.com
PO Box 156
Corvallis, MT 59828
406/961.1900

"We are both inspired by beautiful combinations of color in nature, finished artwork or garments"

Artyarns

What's a designer to do if they want to write a book about knitting with luxury yarn, but can't find the yarns they have in mind? If you're Iris Schreier, designer extraordinaire, you ask your engineer husband to develop equipment that will allow you to manufacture exactly what you need. As it turns out, what Iris wanted were the sublime luxury yarns for which Artyarns is now famous.

This creative eye may be genetic for Iris. She comes from a long line of artistic people, including a maternal grandmother who was a couturiere and a paternal great grandmother who owned a yarn shop and taught knitting.

Before Artyarns started manufacturing their own yarn bases, Iris began her dyeing career like most other dyers, making unique yarns by dyeing various white skeins she purchased from other manufacturers in her small studio.

Now, the entire company, including dye studio, yarn manufacturing space, and business offices, is located in a large factory space in White Plains, New York.

What Sets This Company Apart
Artyarns creates their own unique yarn bases. They are known for their stunning colorways and exceptional fiber combinations.

Contact Info
www.artyarns.com
sales@artyarns.com

"We bring couture luxury and elegance to hand knitting."

Owners: Iris & Elliot Schreier

Date Established: 2003

Location: White Plains, New York

Favorite Color: red

Favorite Book: *The Girl with the Dragon Tattoo* by Stieg Larsson

Favorite Movies: *American Gangster* and *The Departed*

Hobbies: all needlecrafts, beading, hiking and weight lifting

Featured Yarn: Cashmere Sock

Colorway: *#168*

Owners: Robin & Chuck Page

Date Established: 2005

Location: San Pedro, California

Favorite Color: "harvesty"colors

Favorite Movie: *Urban Cowboy*

Hobby: rug hooking

Featured Yarn: Alyeska

Colorway: *Lavender Fields*

Inspiration: As the name suggests, it was inspired by a field of lavender.

Pagewood Farm

Robin Page is a woman of many fiber-related talents. It was at a quilt market in Houston, Texas, where she saw someone spinning and decided she would like to give it a try. When she got back to Los Angeles, she found a spinning wheel and teacher. Very soon after, she began her spinning career in earnest.

She soon found that it was difficult to find spinning fiber in Southern California, so she began purchasing natural-colored fiber on Ebay.com and dyeing it herself. She was already an experienced dyer from years of rug hooking, with skills that were directly transferable.

Robin proved to be a quick study and soon had more handspun, hand-dyed yarn than she or her friends needed, so she and her husband began selling it to yarn shops. Those that didn't buy from her suggested that she start dyeing commercially-spun yarns that would better suit their budgets. She took that advice and, over time, Pagewood Farm transformed into the business it is today.

Robin now spends 12+ hour days in her covered outdoor studio managing all aspects of the company, including a team of sales reps who service her wholesale customers.

What Sets This Company Apart
Pagewood Farm has a dye technique Robin feels is unlike any she has seen used at other companies. She is constantly seeking new products that help them stand out from other hand-dyers, including needle felting scarf kits and their "Handspun Bouquet" yarns.

Contact Info
www.pagewoodfarm.com
orders@pagewoodfarm.com

"I learned from teachers who taught me to not be afraid of trying and that anything could be resurrected."

LavenderSheep

Yvonne Ellsworth has been fortunate to be surrounded by innovative, interesting women her entire life. One of her fondest childhood memories is of her mother sketching and sewing exquisite wedding dresses at their dining room table.

Yvonne credits her grandmother with teaching her to crochet and knit, and with setting her on the path to her fiber-filled career. Her grandmother was always doing something fiber-related, including spinning, weaving and knitting. After she taught Yvonne to knit at age 15, she introduced her to her first knitting circle.

This dynamic, supportive group of women encouraged Yvonne to become involved with the fiber studies program at the University of Oregon. While working on her business degree, Yvonne starting taking weaving classes for fun. Her professors covered yarn dyeing in their weaving courses, and Yvonne was hooked. From then on, she took every course she could find that included dyeing and surface design.

Ultimately, Yvonne graduated with a degree in business with a focus in entrepreneurship, and art with a focus in textiles. From the start, she and her husband planned for her to run a home-focused business. This meshed well with yarn dyeing, and LavenderSheep was born.

Now her days are filling with dyeing in her home studio, running all of the other aspects of her business, and taking care of her young family.

What Sets This Company Apart

Bright colorways inspired by the beauty of the Columbia River Gorge, and a wide variety of base yarns and fibers, ranging from silk lace yarn to bulky nylon ribbon yarn.

Contact Info

www.lavendersheep.com
PO Box 295
Cascade Locks, OR 97014

"From the time I was really small, I have been interested in textiles."

Owner: Yvonne Ellsworth

Date Established: 2007

Location: Cascade Locks, Oregon

Favorite Color: Purple

Favorite Books: *Pride and Prejudice*, a little sci-fi, and fantasy. "I like interesting plot lines with characters you get to know and relatively happy endings"

Hobbies: occassionally sewing, but mostly dyeing, spinning and knitting

Featured Yarn: Tencel Sock

Colorways: *Owenburger, Mountain Sunset*

Inspiration: The *Owen* colorway was inspired by Chrissy's son, whose favorite color is blue. *Mountain Sunset* plays on the rich pinks that surround Yvonne's beloved Mount Hood at sunset.

Owner: Dianne E. Lutz

Date Established: 2006

Location: Greer, South Carolina

Favorite Color: red

Favorite Book: *Mr. Perfect* by Linda Howard

Hobbies: reading, running

Featured Yarn: Steele

Colorway: *String Thing*

Inspiration: This colorway was an experiment using the same colors but a different technique to apply them to the yarn.

Creatively Dyed

Soon after Dianne Lutz opened her yarn shop, Yarns Forever, in 2005, it became apparent that she would need to do something to set herself apart if she wanted her shop to succeed. It seemed to her that all the other yarn shops in the area carried the same yarn lines and were only competing with each other through their various sales.

Dianne decided that she would be different by carrying her own exclusive yarn line. Since she'd already been selecting yarn for her shop, she was familiar with the kinds of base yarns she liked, namely high-quality fibers that would last for years. She had some training in hand-dyeing, as well as the support of many other hand-dyers, and felt confident taking the plunge.

Now Dianne spends much of her time on the road, selling her hand-dyes at fiber shows. Creatively Dyed makes 90% of its income from fiber festivals around the country.

When not on the road, Dianne spends long days in her studio, which is in the basement of her home. She has ten burners, used for setting her yarn, and four bookshelves full of various dyes. There is a large area for drying yarn and four large tables used for dye application. Like all of the other fiber artists in this book, Dianne applies the dye by hand to each skein she sells.

What Sets This Company Apart
Unique dyeing techniques unlike any others. Her exciting color sense is inspired by the costumes and decorations of Carnival in her native Trinidad and Tobago.

Contact Info
www.creativelydyed.net
info@creativelydyed.net

"A typical day in my studio is nothing like my previous job as a computer programmer. I'm not one of the dyers who have a set way of dyeing and dye the same way and colors every single time."

Black Bunny Fibers

Like so many fiber-related businesses, Black Bunny Fibers started off simply. Carol, an attorney turned stay-at-home mom, began with a blog. Among the things she wrote about were her experiments with hand-dyeing. First, she played with Kool-Aid brand drink, then quickly switched to acid dyes. She received such enthusiastic encouragement from her blog readers that she decided to try selling her hand-dyed yarn on Etsy.com.

Carol has since moved her business to her own web site and has expanded to include hand-dyed fiber and her own knitting patterns. She has even written a couple of books, including one about knitting with hand-painted yarns.

Carol still dyes all of her yarn and fiber in her 1970's kitchen, complete with Harvest Gold linoleum. While she would like to carve out some actual studio space at some point in the future, for now she sees this as a positive thing because it allows her to be in the heart of her home, right in the middle of the action with her family.

Among these family members is the black bunny for whom the company is named. Charcoal, a Lionhead Rabbit who lives in Carol's kitchen, is too small to contribute fiber to the company himself. Instead, he does his part by supervising Carol's work

What Sets This Company Apart

Carol has very few set colorways. She loves to experiment with different colors and combinations. In addition to staving off boredom, this allows her to "keep things fresh, inspiring and enticing". Carol's yarn club members do not get swag or patterns, but instead receive yarn or fiber that has been dyed to their specific color preferences.

Contact Info

www.blackbunnyfibers.com

"I give a lot of individual attention to each skein or batch of fiber, and I think this shows in the end result"

Owner: Carol J. Sulcoski

Date Established: 2006

Location: Villanova, Pennsylvania

Favorite Color: "Really impossible to answer, especially since becoming a hand-dyer has taught me to appreciate all colors, even ones I'm not intuitively drawn to. "

Hobbies: reading, gardening, quilting and sewing, cooking

Featured Yarn: Superwash Merino Classic

Colorway: *Kathy's Cape*

Inspiration: "*Kathy's Cape* was named after a friend (Kathy Elkins of WEBS) who wrote beautifully about her love of the ocean while on Cape Cod. I wanted to play with a semi-solid blue with green in it, catching the way the ocean sometimes looks in the sunshine."

Owners: Laura Lough & Kelly Eells

Date Established: 2007

Location: Trinity, North Carolina

Favorite Color: Laura - greens and earth tones; Kelly - all of them!

Hobbies: Laura - working on her small farm with her sheep, chickens and garden; Kelly - working out, listening to audio books and podcasts

Featured Yarn: Verve

Colorway: *Firestarter*

Inspiration: "I have always been a fan of fantasy novels and a common character in fantasy is the 'fire starter', or pyrokinetic (i.e. someone who can start and/or control fires with his or her mind). This was on my mind when I created this fiery colorway! "

The Unique Sheep

Laura Lough started dyeing yarn for herself and her friends when she was in college. As graduation neared, she realized it was time to decide on a career, but found that her degree in anthropology and gender studies wasn't terribly practical. She'd enjoyed her earlier yarn dyeing experiences, so she decided to start a hand-dyed yarn company.

About a year later, after The Unique Sheep had officially been in business for just a few months, Kelly Eells joined Laura as a business partner. That's when the company really started to gain momentum.

Before joining The Unique Sheep, Kelly dyed yarn under the business name Liisu Yarns. Running Liisu on her own, Kelly was kept too busy to develop any of the great ideas she had swirling around in her mind. Once she joined Laura at The Unique Sheep, she finally had the time needed to develop what would eventually become the Gradience technique, for which the company is best known.

Now both Laura and Kelly are able to work out of studios in their own homes, with the occasional overflow into the rest of the house. Both say they are thankful to have such understanding and supportive husbands.

What Sets This Company Apart
Their Gradience colorways are created in such a way that as the knitter works from one skein to the next (colorways generally come in sets of four to six small skeins), the color gradually changes.

Contact Info
www.theuniquesheep.com
laura@theuniquesheep.com
kelly@theuniquesheep.com

"Some of our best selling colors come from customer requests. We love collaboration and are always eager to put exactly the right color in our customer's hands."

Abstract Fiber

Susan Stambaugh is not afraid of color - anyone who has ever seen her dazzling yarns and fibers knows this. What you might not realize is that Susan's yarn is an extension of the color palette she surrounds herself with all the time.

This relationship with color has deep roots. Susan started her crafting life as a quilter. The quilts that hang in her home are full of vibrant color and a familiar palette of bright reds, hot pinks, turquoise, blues, greens and oranges.

In order to make these lovely quilts, Susan was always on the lookout for bright colored silk and cotton threads. Susan eventually took a four-day thread dyeing class in Seattle, where she learned how to create exactly the thread colors she needed.

Not long after, she started spinning yarn and decided to try dyeing her own fiber. Her first attempt at selling her hand-dyed fiber was at the annual 'Ides of March' parking lot sale at a Portland, Oregon, yarn shop. The following year, she participated in the same sale and added another event. Sandi, the buyer for another local yarn shop, Knit Purl, asked if she had ever thought about dyeing yarn, and the rest is history.

In the meantime, Susan continued with her career in real estate. She was raised in a family that valued financial stability over following your passion, so she wanted to be very sure of where Abstract Fiber was going before she quit. She finally felt comfortable leaving her day job in 2009.

These days, Susan, her production dyer and right hand, Karen, and their employees spend their days dyeing yarn in Susan's studio, which has taken over her entire basement. It only occasionally spills upstairs and onto the dining room table.

What Sets This Company Apart
Aside from their bold palette, they guarantee no knots in their skeins. They also employ a dyeing technique that minimizes pooling and striping.

Contact Info
www.abstractfiber.com

"Color is my art."

Owner: Susan Stambaugh

Date Established: 2007

Location: Portland, Oregon

Number of Employees: 3

Favorite Colors: "Anything rich. More is better. How could I choose?"

Favorite Movie: *Good Will Hunting*

Favorite Book: *The Tennis Partner* by Abraham Verghese

Hobbies: cooking, training Portuguese Water Dogs, gardening, spinning, quilting

Featured Yarn: Supersock

Colorway: *Portland*

Inspiration: "The roses in my garden."

Owner: Tina Newton

Date Established: 1991

Location: Scappoose, Oregon

Number of Employees: 5

Favorite Color: loves them all and how they work together

Favorite Movie: *Love Actually*

Favorite Book: *Sister Stories* by Brenda Peterson

Hobbies: spinning, weaving

Featured Yarn: Socks That Rock Mediumweight

Colorway: *Scum Bubbles*

Inspiration: Part of the "scummy" series, all inspired by the various permutations of scum on water. Tina loves complicated colors with lots of shading, and this series fits into that category.

Blue Moon Fiber Arts

Tina Newton, founder of Blue Moon Fiber Arts, grew up left-handed in a right-handed world. She spent her young life wishing she could knit and crochet like the other crafty women in her family, but was told her left-handedness meant she couldn't be taught.

When she grew up, she decided that maybe she could learn to crochet and signed up for a class at Northwest Wools in Portland, Oregon. Her teacher, it turned out, was also a lefty and had Tina knitting and crocheting in minutes.

Tina also learned to spin and fell "head over heels in love". At the time, there weren't very many hand-dyed rovings on the market, so she thought she would give dyeing her own a try. She took a few classes, but mainly read books and learned through trial and error. She worked to understand the chemistry and then experimented until she started to get results she liked.

One day, as Tina was spinning some of her hand-dyed roving, she was approached by an admiring fellow spinner who bought everything Tina had with her. This same women remains a Blue Moon customer today.

At the time of this chance meeting, Tina was working as a therapist but ready to make a change. She started successfully selling her hand-dyed roving and hand-spun yarn at small shows.

All the awe-inspiring things that are now Blue Moon Fiber Arts followed, including custom-milled sock yarn and their wildly popular sock clubs. Most recently, Tina started the event production company Knot Hysteria (the force behind the giant sock knitting gathering Sock Summit) with her friend Stephanie Pearl-McPhee.

What Sets This Company Apart

Very precise recipes that result in consistent quality and reliably excellent products, no matter which Blue Moon dyer creates them.

Contact Info

info@bluemoonfiberarts.com
www.bluemoonfiberarts.com

"I can never run out of colors. I love to challenge myself with color."

CraftsMeow

We have all heard the quote "when life give you lemons, you make lemonade". When life gave Gwen Clark lemons, she likes to say she made lemon sorbet. After many years of managing payrolls for various organizations, she lost her job. Unfortunately, this was in January 2009, a time when many people found themselves in the same situation and there were not enough jobs to go around.

One day, as Gwen was consoling herself while knitting a sock, she realized that the yarn she was using, white with splotches of brown and pink, looked like Neapolitan ice cream. Her next thought was, "I could make this!" She checked out every dyeing book she could get from the library, ordered some inexpensive wool yarn and purchased some dye. She then set about teaching herself to dye yarn.

After a few false starts and lots of learning experiences, she produced some sample yarns that her family and friends loved. She began selling her products on Etsy.com, at knitting shows around the country, and via a growing wholesale business.

Gwen dyes all of her yarn in her family's kitchen, drying it out on her deck. This arrangement works well, as long as it is a dry, non-windy day. If not, she dries the yarn in her bathroom, which can take days. She skeins yarn at her dining room table and uses one of her bedrooms as an office to run the business aspects of CraftsMeow.

Although this enterprise has taken over much of their home, her family remains "100% supportive", even helping her at shows.

What Sets This Company Apart
Dessert-themed colorways, coordinated mini-skeins, and a focus on fingering weight yarns

Contact Info
craftsmeow.etsy.com
CraftsMeowYarnStudio@cox.net

"My passion: sweet, delicious desserts that don't increase the size of my waistline."

Owner: Gwen Clark

Date Established: 2009

Location: Glendale, Arizona

Favorite Color: pink

Favorite Movies: *The Sound of Music* and *Pretty Woman*

Hobbies: scrapbooking, Facebook, used to foster kittens but that does not go well with all of the yarn now filling the house!

Featured Yarn: Soft Serve

Colorway: *Witch's Brew*

Inspiration: "Halloween is my favorite holiday and I thought it would be very cool to have socks in Halloween colors. Purple, black, and orange seemed perfect for Halloween and *Witch's Brew* was born."

Owner: Lorajean Kelley

Date Established: 2007

Location: Portland, Oregon

Favorite Color: "I think shades of color is my favorite color!"

Favorite Book: *Half the Sky* by Nicholas Kristof and Sheryl WuDunn

Hobbies: parenting two small boys, outdoor activities

Featured Yarn: Superwash Merino Fingering

Colorway: *Ladies That Lunch*

Inspiration: "Back when I worked in restaurants I had a few girlfriends that worked around town at different places. We'd get dressed up and go have lunch at each others restaurants. We considered ourselves to be 'Ladies that Lunched'. There might have been a few cocktails involved."

Knitted Wit

Lorajean Kelley, owner of Knitted Wit, is a strong believer in community and the power of women working together. Community has played an important part in the development and success of her business from the start.

Lorajean began dyeing yarn with her friend, Helen Hulskamp of Painted Skeins, when they couldn't find the specific products they wanted on the market. They learned together, each drawing on their own personal strengths. Selling their surplus to pay for more yarn and fiber was a natural next step. While getting Knitted Wit up and running, Lorajean called upon her experience as assistant manager at a fair trade retail shop.

As Knitted Wit continued to grow, Lorajean moved into a large studio space shared with Stevanie Pico and Deb Accuardi of the now-defunct Pico Accuardi Dyeworks. They traveled to shows together and collaborated on a number of projects, growing their businesses in concert. This relationship was great for both companies and really helped to establish Knitted Wit as an integral part of the larger fiber-related community in the Pacific Northwest.

Great customer service and a fun, sassy attitude are a huge part of what makes a visit to Lorajean's dye space, online store or the Knitted Wit booth at fiber shows so much fun.

What Sets This Company Apart
A bright, playful palette of interesting candy-colored mixes.

Contact Info
www.knittedwit.com
info@knittedwit.com

"I am a big believer in community. I have learned so much from other women in the fiber arts community and I wouldn't be here without them."

Cephalopod Yarns

Sarah Eyre is an avid photographer who takes highly detailed photographs of color, shape and texture. She is also a dedicated painter and knitter. A number of years ago, she started seeing articles about hand-painted yarns and the idea appealed to her. For Sarah, photography and painting have always been more about the colors and the process than the actual subject. Combining her passion for visual arts with her love of knitting seemed like a winning idea.

She jumped right in, working with acid dyes immediately, and delighted in the experience. She quickly amassed a trove of delectable hand-dyed yarn and decided to start selling it so that others could share in the enjoyment. She was able to use the money earned from these sales to buy more yarn to dye. It was a fulfilling, sustainable cycle.

To make the transition to self-employment possible, Sarah took a year off from her corporate job and went to Afghanistan to work as a translator. This allowed her to pay off her debts and start her life as an indie dyer in earnest.

In 2008, Sarah joined forces with Gryphon Perkins to run the enormously popular Sanguine Gryphon. In late 2011, Sanguine Gryphon was very amicably dissolved, with both Sarah and Gryphon starting their own independent ventures.

Now Sarah is eagerly looking forward to growing Cephalopod Yarns, working with the people and processes she adores.

What Sets This Company Apart
Ethically-sourced, custom-milled yarn in luxury fiber combinations painted in deep, opulent colorways.

Contact Info
www.cephalopodyarns.com
Cephalopod Yarns on Facebook
1547 Ridgley Street, Suite B
Baltimore, MD 21230
410/528.8660

"It is beautiful to be part of others' creative process."

Owner: Sarah Eyre

Date Established: 2011, formerly part of The Sanguine Gryphon

Location: Easton, Maryland

Number of Employees: 10

Favorite Color: changes with the seasons

Favorite Movie: *Harold and Maude*

Hobbies: photography, yoga, running, painting, coloring books, hiking, cat wrangling, playing the banjo (very badly)

Featured Yarn: Bugga

Colorway: *Question Mark Butterfly*

Blue Ridge Yarns

Owner: Leanna Witt

Date Established: 2007

Location: Amissville, Virginia

Favorite Color: green

Favorite Movie: *Down Periscope*

Hobbies: gardening, spinning, weaving, biking and kayaking

Featured Yarn: Footprints

Colorway: *Mossy Hollow*

Inspiration: "There is a wooded area at the back of the farm, that has a beautiful creek and lots of little water runs trickling into it. As we walked through there one day, we noticed a shady slope covered with moss and pretty little dark pink flowers. Even the doggies stopped to take a look!"

Just after Leanna Witt was born, her mother founded Misty Mountain Farm and began to raise Finnsheep, Angora goats and Angora rabbits. The business eventually expanded into selling hand-dyed yarns and fibers. Leanna grew up helping with the business and attending fiber festivals. As you might expect, she grew to love a multitude of fiber arts from an early age. She started with spinning and knitting, then felting, and finally started weaving at the ripe old age of 14.

After college, Leanna returned home and was helping her mother with her business when she realized this was something she, too, would love to make her career. She jumped in with both feet and started her wholesale business with a booth at the June 2007 TNNA show. She left that show with a stack of orders, a list of sales reps and a clear idea that this was going to work.

Now Leanna spends her days in her studio, a converted three-car garage, where she dyes yarn and fills orders. She has her office space, dye space, and storage all together, with cabinets and shelves to keep it organized. She is able to watch the alpacas and sheep while she works, and is occasionally interrupted by the guinea hens, who come to her door looking for a snack.

What Sets This Company Apart
Innovative packaging ideas, such as sock yarns with smaller skeins of coordinating solid yarns for toes and heels, and larger variety packs for her retailers.

Contact Info
www.blueridgeyarns.com
PO Box 133
Amissville, VA 20106
540/937.4707

"I try to be innovative and flexible, coming up with new colors, yarns, and pattern support."

Lorna's Laces

Lorna's Laces was started back in the 1990's by Lorna Miser, in Placerville, California. It was very successful, but by 2002, Lorna was ready to move on and she put the company up for sale.

This is where Beth Casey enters the picture. As Lorna was starting Lorna's Laces, Beth was working in college textbook publishing and, over time, becoming very bored. At the urging of her husband, Beth left publishing only to spend the next few years searching for the right fit. During this time, she "... studied bread baking at the French Culinary Institute in New York, walked dogs, and watched way too much daytime TV."

One day, while looking through a knitting magazine, Beth noticed a tiny ad near the back for a hand-dyeing business that was available for purchase. She called, and the rest is history.

After learning to dye from Lorna, Beth moved the company to Chicago, where it resides in a 2400 square foot warehouse building in the Ravenswood neighborhood.

Now all of Beth's days are spent working with people she cares about, making products she loves.

What Sets This Company Apart

Lorna's Laces is all about enticing colors and classic fibers. They work very hard to make sure that their work is consistent and reliable on both the product and customer service fronts. Also, they never retire a colorway!

Contact Info

www.lornaslaces.net
4229 N Honore St
Chicago, IL 60613
773/935.3803
yarn@lornaslaces.net

"We create beautiful yarn by hand every day so that, in turn, knitters can create something beautiful by hand for a loved one. I believe that whether we knit for ourselves, a family member or a total stranger, we stitch love into every finished product."

Owner: Beth Casey

Date Established: 1990s

Location: Chicago, Illinois

Favorite Color: orange

Favorite Movie: *Good Will Hunting*

Favorite Books: *To Kill a Mockingbird* by Harper Lee, *The Giant's House* by Elizabeth McCracken, *A Confederacy of Dunces* by John Kennedy Toole and *Geek Love* by Katherine Dunn

Hobbies: cooking and running

Featured Yarn: Shepherd Sock

Colorway: *Retro Soda*

Inspiration: These are Chrissy Gardiner's favorite colors!

Abbreviations

C2B: Sl1 to cable needle and hold in back, k1, k1 from cable needle

C2F: Sl1 to cable needle and hold in front, k1, k1 from cable needle

C4B: Sl2 to cable needle and hold in back, k2, k2 from cable needle

C4F: Sl2 to cable needle and hold in front, k2, k2 from cable needle

CC: contrasting color

dpn(s): double-pointed needle(s)

k: knit

k2tog: knit 2 stitches together

k3tog: knit 3 stitches together

k-fb: knit in front and back of same stitch (increase 1 stitch)

k-fbf: knit in front, back and front of same stitch (increase 2 stitches)

k-tbl: knit stitch through back loop

m1: make a stitch by picking up strand between two stitches and knitting it tbl

m1p: make a stitch by picking up strand between two stitches and purling it tbl

MC: main color

p: purl

p2tog: purl 2 stitches together

pm: place marker

psso: pass slipped stitch over

p-tbl: purl stitch through back loop

pu: pick up and knit

RS: right side

sl: slip stitch as if to purl

sl-left: sl3, pass 3rd stitch on right needle over first two stitches and off needle, slip those two stitches back to left needle, k1, YO, k1

sl-right: pass 3rd stitch to the left on left needle over first two stitches and off needle, k1, YO, k1

S2KP: slip 2 stitches together as if to knit, k1, pass 2 slipped stitches over

SK2P: slip 1 stitch as if to knit, knit next two stitches together, psso

SSK: slip 2 stitches one at a time as if to knit, insert left needle tip into the front of the two stitches and knit them together

T2B: Sl1 to cable needle and hold in back, k1, p1 from cable needle

T2F: Sl1 to cable needle and hold in front, p1, k1 from cable needle

T3B: Sl1 to cable needle and hold in back, k2, p1 from cable needle

T3F: Sl2 to cable needle and hold in front, p1, k2 from cable needle

T4B: Sl2 to cable needle and hold in back, k2, p2 from cable needle

T4F: Sl2 to cable needle and hold in front, p2, k2 from cable needle

tbl: through back loop(s)

WS: wrong side

W&T: wrap and turn

WY: waste yarn

wyib: with yarn in back

wyif: with yarn in front

x: repeat 'x' times

YO: yarn over

YO 2x: yarn over twice (results in two stitches on needle)

| |: slip marker

Kitchener stitch:

To prepare stitches for Kitchener stitch, place half of the stitches on one needle and half on the other with the needles parallel to where the seam will ultimately be.

Cut the yarn leaving a 12" to 16" tail. Thread the tail on a yarn needle and position the needles so that the working yarn is coming off of the right end of the back needle.

Step 1: Insert yarn needle into first stitch on front needle as if to purl and pull through, leaving stitch on needle.

Step 2: Insert yarn needle into first stitch on back needle as if to knit and pull through, leaving stitch on needle.

Step 3: Insert yarn needle into first stitch on front needle as if to knit and pull through, slipping stitch off needle.

Glossary of Techniques

Step 4: Insert yarn needle into second stitch on front needle as if to purl and pull through, leaving stitch on needle.

Step 5: Insert yarn needle into first stitch on back needle as if to purl and pull through, slipping stitch off needle.

Step 6: Insert yarn needle into second stitch on back needle as if to knit and pull through, leaving stitch on needle.

Repeat Steps 3 - 6 until a single stitch remains on each needle, then work Steps 3 and 5 to complete the seam. Thread yarn tail to WS of work and weave in end to finish seam.

lift wrap RS:

Using tip of right needle, lift wrap from the front of the wrapped stitch (or RS of work) and put it on the left needle behind the wrapped stitch, essentially unwrapping it. Then, knit the wrap and its corresponding stitch together through their back loops.

lift wrap WS:

Using tip of right needle, lift wrap from the back of the wrapped stitch (or RS of work) and put it on the left needle behind the wrapped stitch, essentially unwrapping it. Then, purl the wrap and its corresponding stitch together.

m1/m1-pwise:

To increase using the m1 or "make one" method, lift the bar between the needles with the right needle tip, inserting it from back to front. Place the bar on the left needle and knit it through the back loop.

To increase using the m1-pwise method, lift the bar between the needles with the right needle tip, inserting it from back to front. Place the bar on the left needle and purl it through the back loop.

pick up stitch:

To pick up a stitch, insert the tip of the right needle into the knitting from RS to WS in the spot where you need the extra stitch. Wrap the yarn around the needle as if you are knitting and pull up a loop.

reverse stockinette:

This is the back side of stockinette stitch. When working flat, purl the right side rows and knit the wrong side rows.

stockinette stitch:

This term is commonly used to refer to smooth knitted fabric. When working in the round, knit every round to produce stockinette. When working flat, knit the right side rows and purl the wrong side rows.

W&T on RS:

Sl1, bring yarn to front of work between needles, sl same stitch back to left needle, bring yarn to back of work between needles, turn work. Yarn is wrapped around base of stitch that was just slipped back and forth. This stitch should not have been worked in the process.

W&T on WS:

Sl1, bring yarn to back of work between needles, sl same stitch back to left needle, bring yarn to front of work between needles, turn work. Yarn is wrapped around base of stitch that was just slipped back and forth. This stitch should not have been worked in the process.